# The 7 Habits
# Of
# Highly Miserable
# People

## And How To Avoid Them!

by
Mark D. Borup, M.D.

## Authors Choice Press
New York   Lincoln   Shanghai

## The 7 Habits of Highly Miserable People

Authors Choice Press
an imprint of iUniverse, Inc.

For information address:
iUniverse, Inc.
2021 Pine Lake Road, Suite 100
Lincoln, NE 68512
www.iuniverse.com

ISBN: 0-595-24709-1

Printed in the United States of America

Dedicated to

Calene,
who helps me keep
my demons at bay,

and to

Roy,
the most miserable
person I've ever known.

# CONTENTS

# Chapter 10
Habit #6: Resent the Unfairness

# Chapter 11
Habit #7: Avoid the Present Moment

# Chapter 12
Avoiding the Seven Habits

# 1

# Royalties and Other Reasons Why I Wrote This Book

Today, many Americans are, to varying degrees, acquainted with misery, even those who have never had to sit through an entire Ice Capades show or attend a Monster Truck Pull event. How many of us have found ourselves feeling the full weight of human existence, its meaninglessness, its cruel indifference, its pervasive unsatisfactoriness and then, rather than continue to ponder these issues, we instead reached for the remote control button to change the channel in order to lose ourselves in all the intrigue of the last half of a *Matlock* rerun? I know I have, and on more than one occasion. What is the source of such deep discontent, powerful enough to drive us to such incredibly desperate means of distracting ourselves from our own misery? Often to the point of spending several hours hypnotized in front of a TV watching the World Federation Wrestling network. And, thus, rather than dealing with the weightier matters of our existence, we chose instead to spend our time wondering whether those wrestling matches are real or staged? Or perhaps some combination of real and staged?

In *Walden*, Thoreau recognized that the "mass of men lead lives of quiet desperation."* This insight seems to be just as true today, except that people nowadays often choose louder means of expressing their desperation. Sometimes too loud, as when the tremendous stress of hand-sorting envelopes by zip codes leads a person to such a level of disgruntlement that that same person may go as far as joining the N.R.A or some equally senseless act that flies in the face of all rational thinking, common sense and good judgement. But what is the source of this widespread feeling of desperation and malcontent? Is it the natural state of human beings to be miserable and dissatisfied? Why are we so quick to surrender to such bland distractions as electronic gadgetry, movie sequels, celebrity gossip magazines, and TV game shows like *Who Wants to Be a Millionaire?* Have we given up all hope of ever being able to achieve true happiness and joy in our lives? Might finding happiness truly be, as some modern psychologists have suggested, more difficult than setting up a really good stereo home theater system? Why do many of us devote more, time and energy trying to get a really fast Internet connection than we do trying to get peace of mind?

Plagued by such disturbing questions, I thus became obsessed with finding the path to true happiness and solving other critical questions of modern day existence (i.e., what the hell are Pokemons and why should I feel I have to "catch 'em all"?). I made a solemn oath to tirelessly search for the answers to these questions and told myself that there was not enough Prozac in the entire state of California to divert me from my goal. Unfortunately, after about three weeks of trying very hard, I was totally discouraged and decided to give up my quest. What did I know about happiness, for Pete's sake? I knew nothing of happiness and contentment. I was married

*Although this statement is probably true, one should question the validity of any statement found in a book documenting a man's two year experience in the wild that lacks any mention of being eaten alive by mosquitoes or longing desperately for a good home-cooked meal after feasting on a charred chipmunk-on-a-stick!*

with three young children, after all. I felt frustrated, generally discouraged, and decided to double up on my dose of Prozac.

But I found that even increasing my daily dose of Prozac was to no avail. I certainly didn't feel any happier. I must admit, however, that, thanks to the magic of Prozac, I did feel more outgoing and sociable and was able to share my discontent more readily with other people. I did take a small degree of solace in knowing that, through the modern miracle of psychopharmacology, I could escape from Thoreau's quietly desperate mass by being transformed into an artificially disinhibited, socially-outgoing malcontent! Thank God for Elli Lilly! No more quiet desperation for me, by damn, as long as I didn't forget to take my medication!

Then last summer, while driving my family down to Disneyland in a minivan, for some reason, I found myself thinking constantly about misery, and I had some of the initial insights that would become the foundation of this book. It all came to fruition as I rode on the "It's A Small World" ride with my four-year-old daughter for the fourth time (in a row). It was something of an epiphany experience, one that hit me squarely in the gut, harder than a bad hotdog! Misery! That was a concept I knew more intimately than Sigfried knows Roy. I didn't just know about misery, I lived it. Misery in my life was like a Visa card: it was everywhere I wanted to be. I was a virtual misery guru. And what do gurus do? They write self-help books, of course.

The concept was simple. Most people never really find meaning or happiness in their lives and simply resign themselves to all the mindless distractions of modern life (daytime TV drama, for example) in order to help make the time pass by a bit quicker. But they continue to dream of one day being content, and this often causes them to waste time and energy on what ends up being an unattainable goal anyway. But what if, I wondered to myself, people had a self-help book that taught them the most efficient and direct path to misery, a path that could streamline the whole process, by detailing the seven most common habits found in miserable people? Armed with such knowledge, people could resign themselves more quickly to their miserable, meaningless existence and get on with the business of engaging in the shallow distractions that end up consuming the vast majority of their lives anyway. I marveled at the incredible simplicity of this concept.

But before I could finish marveling at the brilliance of this concept, I was immediately struck by another problem: how could I come up with enough content to fill an entire book with such a simple concept? Once again I found myself discouraged. I went home and browsed through several of my many self-help books. It was then that I realized a key feature that almost all popular self-help books have in common: namely that despite the fact that the authors' general concepts and take-home messages could easily fit on a bumper sticker, the authors are always able to expound on these relatively simple concepts for hundreds of pages! Think about it for a moment! Some of the most popular self-help books (or series of books) are nothing more than overly exhaustive two to three hundred page expositions on simple concepts that could easily be understood fully during a ten-minute lunch discussion! And, after all, the take-home messages from my book concept would require a full seven bumper stickers!

Being a real doctor (and we're talking M.D. here!) I decided to take a rather novel approach, rarely attempted by most self-help gurus. Yes, rather than simply professing the self-evident truth of my enlightened path, I would combine the validating power of carefully thought-out research with my wildly unfounded speculations and conclusions. This is something we doctors refer to as "the scientific method" or as it's more commonly known to the lay public, "the Trident Sugarless Gum Test of Medical Reliability" (i.e., requiring agreement by four out of five doctors). I decided to begin by conducting field research on the topic of misery using a double blind study, which was rather easy since neither my research team nor I had any idea what we were doing.

To begin my study of misery and the habits that lead most directly to it, I decided to closely observe ordinary people. I embarked on my study in New York's Central Park in October 1997 by following people around the park and observing their behavior. This first study, however, ended abruptly after just three weeks, but fortunately, the city's district attorney wasn't able to get the stalking charge to stick and I was released on my own recognizance. Although discouraged, I did learn some valuable lessons from that experience, not the least of which were several practical points of jail etiquette and the true value of soap-on-a-rope.

I next designed a survey study to be conducted within a large city mall. I employed one of those mall survey services and was surprised to learn that many of those mall interviewers do not have criminal records. My survey asked the following questions: 1.) Do you feel, on average, that your life has been, up to this point, miserable and meaningless and if so, why do you think you are miserable? 2.) Do you believe professional wrestling is staged? The results were both surprising and hard to interpret and understand.

Overall, 87% of the people who allowed themselves to be bothered by our staff of pollsters answered either in the affirmative or didn't answer at all but definitely appeared to be quite miserable and were thus scored as if they had answered affirmatively. As expected, among those respondents who were married, the percentage admitting to a miserable existence was a bit higher, at 93%. Interestingly, there was no statistically significant difference when sex was taken into account. People seemed to be just as miserable whether or not they had had sex recently enough to remember when it was. There were also no differences in the prevalence of misery between males and females, although females were found to be much more likely to expound in nauseating detail about the exact causes of their misery, whereas males, when asked this question, were much more likely to just mumble, "Yeah" softly, often with a certain glazed, far-away look in their eyes.

Degree of discontent did correlate positively with age, with more of the older respondents acknowledging that they were miserable, while the younger respondents were more likely to describe themselves as "fine", "OK", and "not too bad, Dude". A few even reported being "happy" on average. From this disparity, we felt justified in concluding that most young people had had too little experience in life to realize just how miserable their lives were. Our finding of a positive direct correlation between misery and I.Q level supported this assumption. The higher the I.Q., the higher the sense of discontent. As the saying goes, ignorance is bliss, and being a bit on the intellectually-challenged side certainly seems to provide some shielding from the truth of one's misery. To misquote Descartes, "I think, therefore I am...miserable". Or something like that.

The tremendous prevalence of folks who believe they lead miserable lives is perhaps not so surprising when one considers the popularity of *The Jerry Springer Show*, but it does beg the obvious question: what is the deal with the 13% of the study group who seem to be either fairly content or at least, unaware of their misery? Naïve stupidity, perhaps? And do these people realize how uncomfortable they make the rest of us 87% feel? And what would it take to educate these people about how truly miserable their mortal existences are? How could they be dissuaded from their delusional belief of being happy and content?

Besides royalties, then, why did I take time away from watching afternoon reruns of *Fantasy Island* to write this book? There are several reasons (including a few I've forgotten) and I'd like to summarize them now. First, the results of my study made me realize that many people start off life rather content, then flounder around, often for decades, before finally having that "ah ha!" experience, when their misery becomes crystal clear to them. And so I wrote this book to provide these people with actual, easy-to-follow guidelines and steps to follow in order to form habits that would more quickly lead them to a fully miserable life. Such a streamlined process would allow us all to get on with our lives and thus get closer to that relief that only death can bring. After all, anything worth doing is worth doing expediently and this applies to living miserably. In addition, I must confess, I wrote this book to convince the aforementioned 13% to see the error of their attitudes and come over to our side of the fence; we, the 87%, Thoreau's quietly desperate mass of men (and women). Misery truly does love company, and the more, the better. It's a given that leading a life of discontent and misery doesn't feel quite so bad when you are able to identify other people who seem to be just as hopeless and miserable, especially when you can convince yourself that their lives are maybe even just a tiny bit more miserable than your own. This truth alone largely explains the popularity of programs like *Judge Judy*, which feature such a Darwinian-challenged segment of the gene pool that few viewers come away from an episode without feeling a bit better about the quality of their own life circumstances!

The Seven Habits described in this book are the fastest and most efficient path to becoming miserable. May your travels along this path be speedy and may you find the truth of your own misery soon.

Before beginning this study of the Seven Habits of highly miserable people, a warning, one that will be repeated over and over in this book, must be stressed:

ALL SEVEN HABITS, IF MISUNDERSTOOD, APPLIED INCORRECTLY, OR OUTRIGHT AVOIDED, COULD LEAD TO A HAPPY AND CONTENT WAY OF LIVING, EVEN TO PEACE OF MIND AND TRUE SERENITY!

This point cannot be over-emphasized. Some unfortunates who might be so bold as to avoid the habits incorporated in this book may actually find their lives enriched. Such misapplication of these habits might even give one a sense of freedom, contentment, and, dare I say it, joyous fulfillment. For such unfortunates, their only course might actually be to live the rest of their lives with relative peace and satisfaction, always separated from fellowship with the rest of us, masses of men living lives of quiet desperation. They remain forever a minority who can't share in the company that true misery provides. The reader should be cautioned, therefore, to take heed in following these steps exactly as they are described in the subsequent chapters of this book. Proceed onward at your own risk!

# 2

# What is Misery And Why Does It Love Company?

Before we begin to learn the Seven Habits of highly miserable living, we should first define misery and look at the history of miserable living. Any reader who has more than three children, can't remember the middle name of their first and second spouses, thinks the guests on *The Ricky Lake Show* remind them of their neighbors and friends, or have worked longer than ten years in the fast food industry can probably skip this chapter. In fact, they probably could stop reading this book, as they are, like the author, well acquainted with misery.

Misery is a word that is a lot like the word "ironic", at least for most of us (Edwin Newman, excused of course): we know what it means when we hear it or see it, but put a gun to our heads and ask any one of us to define it, and, well, I think most of us would soon find ourselves lying motionless on the floor, making a very nasty, hard-to-remove stain on that new carpet we just put in! Fortunately, most of us have escaped the misfortune of such assaults by crazed sociopaths who demand to know the meaning of a word, or else. As part of my study on the prevalence of misery, however, I did ask thousands of people to define what misery meant to them. Below are just a few examples of the responses, obtained without the aid of or

15

under pressure of a handgun. These examples seemed to be fairly representative of the entire sample:

*"Misery is that sometimes vague feeling you have, like, when you're having a really bad hair day."*

*"Misery is that feeling in your stomach when your in-laws inform you that they have decided to stay with you for an extra two weeks."*

*"I feel miserable when I'm really sick or have bad gas."*

*"If you looked up "miserable" in a dictionary, you'd probably see a picture of my husband in the margin"*

*"Misery is getting fired from a job just days before you were going to quit."*

*Misery, much like sh\*t, happens".*

*"Misery is that pervasive sense of hopelessness that fills every pore of your being when you finally wake up from your own self-created delusions of having some kind of meaningful life to realize that you're nothing more than a tiny insignificant nobody, an ant in the infinite cosmos whose actions have less purpose than those knitted cat toilet paper roll consealers that you sometimes see in the back window of large late model Oldsmobiles."*

And then there is this description from Carl Jung (not obtained in the mall survey but lifted entirely out of context from a collection of his writings):

*"...no tangible mood or depression at all, but just a general, dull discontent, a feeling of resistance to everything, a sort of boredom or vague disgust, an indefinable but excruciating emptiness."*

A pretty good description of misery, don't you think? Of course, Carl was referring here to his experience at the Vienna Polka Fest of 1912, but it does sum up the kind of general melancholy we are all familiar with.

As well-educated and intelligent as the good Dr. Jung was, I think the cartoonist who penned the following cartoon captured the true essence of misery and discontent more fully than any of Jung's writings.

Well, I think you get the picture.

# 3

# A Brief History of Misery

Misery has certainly been present since the dawn of man, but most scholars believe that early man was just too stupid to understand how miserable he was. Add to that the fact that there was hardly much time to contemplate one's existence, what, with all the fending off of saber-toothed tigers with rocks and sticks and all. Hence, our prehistoric ancestors found themselves constantly preoccupied with basic survival issues, much like the aspiring young actors living today in New York City or Los Angeles, or like those dancers on the TV drama *Fame*.

Human beings only became aware of how miserable life was when they developed language, because then they had a word for it. That word was "upa", which roughly translated means "that which is akin to or has the characteristics of Mastadon excrement." Most scholars believe that human language itself actually came into existence solely due to the need, within small groups or tribes, to assign the various community tasks and duties to its members, a behavior so vital to a group's survival that it exists even today among married couples and is known as "nagging." It was actually, then, this need to "nag" that brought about the development of human language. And shortly thereafter, early man learned how to stop listening to female tribe members and eventually how to say the early language equivalent of "Not now, dear, I'm watching a really good fight on the tube."

This new behavior of assigning people various tasks within the tribe gave rise to the possibility of societal and cultural misery through the advent of job dissatisfaction. And this most likely occurred shortly after the first tribesman was given the entry-level duty of cleaning Mastodon excrement out of the cave. Competition grew rapidly among tribe members in an attempt to get the best job assignments, like "cave wall painter" or "person to stay back at camp with the women while the others hunt saber-toothed tigers," and within a short time (by geological terms at least) such duty assignment competition led to today's corporate CEOs who make multi-million dollar salaries through generous stock option arrangements. Even though early men had no monetary system within the tribe, tribal women very quickly began to berate their husbands with questions like, "Why do *you* always have to be the tiger bait?" and "Can't you get promoted to a task with better job security, like the cave painter next door?" And suddenly men began to seriously contemplate how it would be if they had a better job (and wife) and women to contemplate how different things would be if their men had better jobs and if they had better husbands. And thus we had the birth of social discontent and misery.

As civilizations developed, man's awareness of misery increased. In early Egyptian society, for example, the vast majority of people were laborers who could only dream of how comfortable and secure the Pharaoh's life must be. This actually gave rise to the first lottery system, in which each laborer was given the opportunity to etch his name onto a small piece of papyrus, place it in a huge clay jar, and hope his name would be drawn at the end of the year. The person whose name was drawn had the opportunity to become the "royal hot water-fetcher" for the royal concubines bath (obviously, the job to have!). This scheme, however, designed solely to help keep the workers' minds off their misery, worked for only a short time. Soon, most of the workers realized that the lottery was fixed because all of the royal water-fetchers had last names like Ramses, Tut, and Pharaohson. Such crude and simple systems of unfair favoritism evolved slowly over time into the more subtle but complex systems of favoritism of today (i.e., organized religion, the U.S. tax code, the governmental bureaucracies of most Asian countries, the Harvard graduate job placement program, and of course, the royal family in England and the Kennedy's and Bush's in America).

The great thinkers of ancient Greek civilization added to man's awareness of misery. Socrates is credited for the usually misquoted warning that the "unexamined life is not worth living."* Not many Greek citizens paid much heed to Socrates' statement, coming as it did from a pedophile who committed suicide and all. But some of the people did begin to examine their lives more closely and thereby came to the obvious conclusion of how miserable their lives, in fact, were. Fearing that such self-examination might lead to civil unrest among the masses, the powers-that-were (the ones with the good jobs) had to find some way to distract the people from dwelling too much on how badly they really had it. And so the Olympic games were born, and with it, the first use of distraction as a means of keeping the "mass of men" from realizing their "desperation", a technique later known as the "Dorothy, Don't Look Behind the Curtain" or the "Smoke and Mirrors" technique used so effectively by American politicians of our day. This concept was similarly employed during the time of the Roman Empire with their gladiator fights, a system which eventually evolved into the National Football League and the World Wrestling Federation of today.

*Originally "The unexamined life is not worth living unless you've got a really good job or the affection of several pretty, young boys."

During the Middle Ages, not much happened in terms of the evolution of misery. Pretty much everyone was extremely miserable, with all the mud and filth, poor dental and general hygiene, thin soups, and all the other general unpleasantry that went along with living in the Middle Ages. The Renaissance, driven largely by a rediscovery of Greek writings and culture, brought about an increased awareness of misery. Although the living conditions of the ancient Greeks were every bit as unpleasant as they had been in the Middle Ages, now everyone could compare their own circumstances with how good it appeared that the ancient Greeks had had it. Imagine, for example, the tremendous amount of perceived misery generated in the minds of middle-aged Europeans when they saw something like Michelanelos' sculpture of David with his buffed washboard abdominals! And then having to hear over and over from their wives, "Why don't *you* have a body like that David guy?" And then consider the dissatisfaction of women who had to hear their husbands complain over and over again, "Why can't you look like that woman in that Rubin's painting? Not eating enough food or what?"

On the other side of the globe, other developments were occurring which had profound effects on our understanding of misery. Perhaps the Buddha contributed more than anyone else in history to our understanding of misery. His statement "Life is suffering", like all real wisdom, is both simple and obvious, and is as true today as it was centuries ago (although the advent of the wheel, indoor plumbing, Spandex gym wear, and Huggies have certainly lessened life's suffering to some degree!). The story of the Buddha's enlightenment is well known and occurred some 2500 years ago. You may recall that the future Buddha was born into a royal family, destined to be a wealthy and powerful king. His father, the king, kept him safely inside the palace walls, to protect him from the ugly

21

realities of life such as sickness, aging, death, and traveling carnival workers. But the young prince, unlike Donny and Marie Osmond, rejected his parental sheltering, and ventured out into the real world, and ironically, actually lived for a time with a group of ascetic "carnies." The Buddha (a name variously translated as either "the Awaked One" or "the One Who Only Sleeps In On Weekends and Holidays") was said to have obtained enlightenment after sitting under a lotus tree for many days. Traditional folklore suggests that the moment of clarity came to him when he realized he had been sitting in a large pile of ox droppings for several weeks, after which he exclaimed, "Life is suffering. But boy, did I have it good back at the palace!" This became the First Noble Truth of the Buddha (later shortened to just "Life is suffering" by his surviving disciples who tired of listening to the Buddha constantly reminiscing about the good old days before leaving his life as a prince to seek enlightenment in the real world). After experiencing enlightenment, the Buddha immediately ran to his closest disciple, Ananda, and proclaimed, "I've been enlightened! Life is suffering!" to which Ananda is said to have replied sarcastically, "No shit, Einstein!" (Scholars still argue about the cause of Ananda's less than receptive state of mind but the two most popular accounts are that he had either 1) just finished discussing a remodeling plan with his famously overweight wife or 2) was in the process of putting together a "some assembly required" bicycle for his son.) In any event, even for those of us who are not Buddhists the concept of life as suffering (or "pervasive unsatisfactoriness", as some would translate "suffering") strikes one as a universal truth, even if he or she has never lived in Arkansas. The First Noble Truth was later restated by John Wayne, who said something to the effect of (I'm paraphrasing now), "Life is difficult. If you're stupid, it's even more difficult!"

Another prophet of misery was Rene Descartes, perhaps most famous for his (oft-misquoted) statement "I think I'm miserable, therefore I am". Descartes had thus discovered that misery is nothing more than a state of mind. This became the basis for his traveling self-help book and seminar tour, in which he urged his fellow Frenchmen to use positive mental attitude techniques to blind themselves to their own miserable conditions. This recipe for self-hypnosis became widely popular throughout France for a number of decades. That is, until the time of the French Revolution, when folks realized that positive mental attitude, while helpful, loses its usefulness once your head has been disconnected from the rest of your body.

In the nineteenth century the Danish thinker Kierkegaard added to our understanding of misery, calling it the "sickness unto death". Thanks to Kierkegaard's ideas, people realized that not only are their lives doomed to be miserable, but, in addition, this misery has absolutely no meaning. As if things could get no worse, along came "Mr. Optimistic" Friedrich Nietzsche, who concluded that all of human history is one big, eternally-repeating cycle without end. So now, thanks to Mr. Nietzsche, we know that rather than having just one ticket for this miserable ride we call "life," it's more like Disneyland and we all have an unlimited pass to continue to ride this thing over and over and over. Forever. Eternally. And if this wasn't bad enough, he also had the audacity to suggest that God was dead. Fortunately, later equally brilliant philosophers deduced that Nietzsche had been wrong on this point, and that God was, in fact, not dead, but had taken indefinite leave from the universe and had not left a forwarding address. Not to mention the fact that He (the Supreme Creator of the Universe) was really, really pissed off at Nietzsche for spreading rumors of His premature death. And so Friedrich, theological sources believe, continues to this day to work closely with his heavenly legal team on an insanity plea that they hope to have ready prior to the Final Judgement.

And so, this concludes a brief historical overview of the concept of misery. We now find ourselves at the beginning of the new millennium living just as miserably as our ancestors before us. Perhaps the only difference is that now, thanks to the miracle of modern technology, we are living miserably at a much more rapid pace. More misery packed into smaller time intervals. Condensed misery, if you will. This is good, in one sense, because we find ourselves today with less free time to ponder how miserable our lives are. Existential issues regarding the meaning of our lives become just another extraneous concern we simply don't have time for! Another modern advance, the Internet, has allowed us to expose ourselves to evidence of other people's misery with the mere click of a mouse, and advances in technology have given us the ability to distract ourselves more efficiently; we find ourselves able to fill every waking minute of our days with distractions from a multitude of convenient gadgets. How fortunate we are to have such wonderful technology! Still, our lives are just as miserable as ever, despite our attempts to distract ourselves from our awareness of it. Could this truly be the endpoint of man's cultural evolution, the seemingly unlimited capacity to produce ever smaller and more convenient means of distracting ourselves from the sad reality of our lives?

# 4

# <u>But Seriously Folks; The Guaranteed Path To Peace of Mind and Serenity</u>

The Seven Habits outlined in this book, if practiced and strictly adhered to, will certainly provide the reader with a foolproof path to a highly miserable life. In fact, these Seven Habits are more than just one way to misery. They provide a roadmap down the most efficient path leading to misery and general discontent. But are any of us truly so masochistic as to deliberately seek out our own misery? While it may be true that misery does love company, I doubt that any of us sets out in life pursuing a life of misery and discontent. Yet the puzzling fact remains: many of us continue to practice many, if not all, of the Seven Habits to varying degrees in our lives. And this fact presents us with an even greater mystery: if nobody deliberately sets out with the goal of creating a miserable life of discontent, why do so many people end up practicing the very habits that invariably lead to such a life? Why do so many of us fail to gain the happiness and security we really want and seek? Sometimes, it seems as if the more we try to obtain happiness, the more elusive it becomes. Are we really capable of escaping misery and discontent? Why are peace of mind, contentedness and true serenity so rare in our day to day lives?

Several months ago I stumbled onto a curious and interesting concept. I was reading a book by the theosophist philosopher Krishnamurti. In this particular book he points out that people often take the wrong tack in their pursuit of desirable character traits. For example, suppose a person wanted to become wise. In such a case the usual, but incorrect, method would be the direct approach, i.e., to focus one's mental energies on trying to be wise. Using this approach, the person in the example would focus directly on wisdom and wise traits, strive to act in wise ways, and in this way attempt to fill his or her self with wisdom. However, if you've ever had the experience of watching someone try to be wise, you probably know the inevitable result; they literally make complete and utter fools of themselves! At least to everyone around them. Krishnamurti concludes that this direct approach to obtain wisdom and become wise is a sure-fire path to foolishness. Instead, Krishnamurti suggested, the best path to wisdom involves concentrating and acknowledging one's *ignorance*. A person truly becomes wise when that person understands and truly acknowledges the things he or she doesn't know, the stupid, irrational thinking errors one makes, the judgements one makes without sound reasoning to back it up, and so forth. Wisdom comes naturally not by trying hard to be wise or by thinking wise thoughts, but rather by deeply understanding, recognizing, and accepting one's ignorance. In this example, Krishnamurti concludes that the goal of wisdom is elusive if attacked straight on or by direct assault, but is best gained by dealing with it's polar opposite.

Krishnamurti goes on to provide another illustrative example. Let's say your goal was to become a perfectly chaste person. One approach, and the one most commonly taken, would be to concentrate all of one's efforts on being virtuous and chaste. Such a person might make up his or her mind to think no unworthy thought and abstain from all unchaste behaviors. What do you think would be the likely result of such an approach for most of us non-saints? Or asked another way, how long do you think most of us would succeed in such a difficult task? Not very long for most of us, maintained Krishnamurti. But what if, he suggested, we took a different tack? What if, instead of trying really hard to be virtuous and chaste, we focused instead on our unchaste tendencies? What if we really acknowledged honestly and openly our own quickness to think and behave in unchaste ways and in this way honestly came to terms with this aspect of ourselves? What Krishnamurti suggested was not to give in to or indulge in one's unchaste tendencies, but simply to acknowledge and identify these tendencies honestly. Such an approach, Krishnamurti believed, would lead a person naturally toward becoming truly chaste.

At the time I discovered it, Krishnamurti's concept seemed to make a lot of sense to me. I wondered whether a similar approach might work in a person's quest for peace of mind and serenity. When I thought about my own failed attempts to get closer to a sense of contentedness, I realized that I had always attempted it by way of a direct frontal assault. As I mentioned earlier, my own experience suggested to me that the harder I tried to be happy, the further away happiness and peace of mind seemed to become. It reminded me of the Buddhist analogy of trying to hunt monkeys by going headlong into the jungle pounding loudly on drums! I wondered if this might be how most people confront the problem of seeking happiness. While I can't say with any certainty, I suspect that it is. It seems to be a part of human nature to attack problems head on! Such an approach leads one to begin with a mental strategy something like this, "Now, let's see. I want to be happy and at peace in my life. What do I need to do (obtain, achieve, procure, etc) to get it?" Isn't this, after all, the typical approach we use? We think with very active verbs and set out to achieve happiness and peace of mind but invariably we give up, frustrated and discouraged when the goal defies our active attempts to obtain it. Often we are left with some thought like, "Obviously, I must not have done it right this time, otherwise I would feel happy (peaceful, serene, or whatever)."

But what if we consider a completely different approach, one that involves beginning with the polar opposite of our goal rather than actively seeking the goal directly? In other words, using Krishnamurti's concept, perhaps the best way to gain more peace of mind and serenity in our lives involves understanding and acknowledging the things we do and the ways in which we think that lead to misery. We would begin this process by identifying the thinking errors and behaviors that directly and invariably lead to misery, insecurity, and unhappiness in our lives. Our first goal would be to understand these habits, not in some abstract or academic sense, but to really understand them in a personal sense. By this, I mean to be cognizant of and acknowledge our own quick tendencies to resort to these habits in our day to day lives. Such an intimate understanding would allow us to readily recognize the very moments we find ourselves slipping into the thought patterns and mindsets that characterize each of these habits. This would allow us the opportunity to immediately say to ourselves, "Oh, here I go trending down the path of the Third Habit (or whichever Habit) and I don't want to go there because I know it leads straight to misery!"

Basically, that's the real premise of this book. Instead of trying our hardest to be happy and content, we might be more successful if we got really good at recognizing the things we do, often unconsciously, that lead to our sense of misery. By avoiding the habits that lead to misery, we should naturally find ourselves more content, with greater peace of mind, and with more serenity. At least most of the time. And what's more, in those moments when we find ourselves feeling miserable, we would then be able to know exactly why we were feeling so miserable. More often, at least. After all, none of us would really enjoy being totally happy 100% of the time! Where's the variety in that? A more reasonable, and obtainable goal would then be to be *mostly* happy, content, and at peace with ourselves *most of the time*.

I hope you will find the following chapters discussing the Seven Habits that lead to misery, both interesting and enjoyable. As you read about each habit, I hope you will try to relate to each habit in a very personal way and recognize your own tendency, however strong or weak, to engage in that particular habit. And then, I hope you will think of examples in your own life where that particular habit has caused you varying degrees of stress, misery, and discontent. If you find yourself not being able to relate to any of the habits, and you don't live in Utah, please e-mail me at mborup@micron.net.

Good luck on the road to discovering and understanding your personal misery! (and thereby, finding peace of mind and joy!)

# 5

# The First Habit:
# Make Yourself the Center of
# the Known Universe!

With this chapter, we begin our discussion of each of the Seven Habits that lead invariably to great misery and discontent. We are about to embark on a kind of personal journey, one in which we will discover our misery. It is perhaps fitting that we pause for a moment to remember the importance of our goal. We should remember that we are not seeking some short-lived, transient life misery (for that, any one of us could simply marry Elizabeth Taylor, and God knows how many of us men have tried that route!). Rather, we seek a profound, undeniable sense of how miserable our lives really are, one that will last a lifetime. Otherwise, why bother?

So our goal should not be taken lightly. It will undoubtedly require lots of hard work and effort. So, how shall we begin?

There is an ancient Chinese proverb that says:

*Every ten thousand-mile journey begins with the first step, so be sure you've got a good pair of shoes with a cushy insole.*

Unknown

This seems to be wise advice to us even today and was certainly even wiser back in the days before the advent of air-cushioned basketball shoes. But how does this pertain to our goal at hand? Why would one need a good pair of shoes before embarking on one's journey toward misery? I've given this a great deal of thought and, frankly, I'm not certain about this one. But I do know this: Before starting off on any kind of journey or trip, its best to eat a good meal, make sure the car is filled with gas, and make any last minute trips to the restroom. In other words (disregarding the last item on that list), you must have fuel, energy, motivation, and drive!

And so, the so-called First Habit, the one discussed in this chapter, is the one that will provide the energy, the fuel, and the drive necessary to propel us down the road toward misery realization. And this is why the first habit is called the First Habit and not the Second Habit. Look at it this way. We need to begin our journey with a source of mental energy and motivation, inexhaustible and easy to replenish, accessible to us all, and one that we are all comfortable and familiar with. What could that source possibly be?

Ask yourself this question; what is the one subject we all think about almost constantly? What single thing do we spend the most energy on and devote the greatest amount of time to? If you haven't figured out the answer yet, I can tell you that the answer is right there in the mirror, staring back at you! Yes, that's right! That object of most importance to you is:

### YOU!

What a wonderful revelation! We begin our journey faced with the problem of finding an inexhaustible source of energy and motivation and, shazam! it turns out that this source is right in front of us! How marvelous! We need look no further than ourselves! Yes, indeed, the strongest force in the universe is your own selfishness. Obi Won Kenobi was right when he said, "The force is within you!" The force of selfishness. And selfishness can become the most powerful force in your life. It is through the First Habit that we will learn to harness this incredible force. The First Habit is stated thusly (for those readers who like bumper sticker slogans):

*Make yourself the center of the known universe!*

Before embarking on the First Habit, however, you, the reader, must be absolutely clear about your goal. For maximum effect, you must imagine yourself as the true center of the universe. It's not enough to imagine that you're "pretty close to the center" or that you're "one of many possible centers" of the known universe. It's also not enough to think that you're "possibly" the center of the universe. Such timid and shaky convictions of one's location in the cosmos will never generate the kind of ultimate selfishness that is necessary to keep one moving toward the goal of ultimate misery. You must become totally convinced that there is only one true geometric center of the universe, that there is room for only one person, and finally, that you, and only you, are, in fact, that very center. In fact, you must believe that your very position marks and defines that center. Anything less than this will not suffice. What we're after here is total self-centeredness, total self-absorption, and total narcissism.

Is such an attitude actually obtainable? Well, consider in your mind, a mental picture of Bruce Willis or Madonna and you'll realize immediately that it's definitely possible! But perhaps you find yourself thinking, "Yes, but I'm not Bruce Willis or Madonna." Fortunately being a self-absorbed celebrity is not a prerequisite for achieving the goal that I'm referring to here. While it does require constant focus, placing yourself at the center of the universe turns out to be a fairly easy thing to do. And, further, it actually becomes easier with time and practice. At first, assuming the position of geometric center of the cosmos may even be somewhat uncomfortable, may feel a little pretentious, some might even say a bit absurd. But when a person spends a few years there, it soon becomes a self-evident fact of the cosmic order. Soon the very idea that there might possibly be other people who actually exist, have feelings, needs, wants, dreams, desires, etc. just like you do, will rarely, if ever, occur to you any more. Such total self-absorption happened for Bruce Willis and Madonna, and it can happen for you!

In the beginning, if you have doubts about being the actual center of the universe, try this simple suggestion. It's actually a technique used in many twelve-step programs and it's stated this way:

FAKE IT, TILL YOU MAKE IT!

Once you've successfully imagined and believe yourself to be the true center, several other equally true cosmic facts will automatically follow:

1. *As the center of the universe, the laws of nature obviously do not apply to you; they do, of course, apply to everyone else in the universe.*

2. *There is no need to be grateful for anything good that might come your way; after all, such things are expected to occur because of your higher place in the cosmic order. The corollary is that any misfortunes that occur in your life become tragedies, literal catastrophes of truly cosmic proportion, which naturally make the misfortunes of others pale in comparison.*

3. *All other people ("non-centers") are merely pawns who play supporting roles in that great cosmic drama that is your life. As*

*Shakespeare said, "All the world's a stage, and we are merely players." This is true, but guess what? You're the director of the play, you're also the central character, and the play is called* The Most Important Life of _____ (insert your full name here).

4. As the center of the universe, your own unique circumstances and personal issues take on a new importance, not only to you, but also to everyone else around you. You are unique and only your problems and concerns are truly real. Anyone who does not share in realizing the gravity of your problems is either stupid or uncaring or both.

And so, the First Habit involves getting in touch with narcissism and self-centeredness. These traits will help us move rapidly along the path toward misery. Now let's try some exercises designed to help us get a firmer grip on the First Habit.

## Daily Affirmations*

1. I am the center of the universe and you're not!

2. I am the Great and Powerful Oz and I'll never let you look behind the curtain!

3. I'm good enough; I'm smart enough, and dog-gone-it, people like me being the center of the universe.

*These should be done at least on a daily basis, in front of a mirror, Stuart Schmalley-fashion.

## Exercises

1. List the three most important reasons why you are the center of the universe*:

a._____

_____

b._____

_____

c._____

_____

*you will probably need more space, so feel free to use additional sheets of paper in order to fully explain your reasons*

2. When a person is talking about him - or herself, use this time to plan your day, to consider the things you need to do to get ahead of other people, etc., all the while pretending that you are listening to and have genuine concern for this individual. This may require some practice at first, but you can actually become quite convincing in this skill.

3. Practice seeing all events, both in your neighborhood and in the world at large, as having meaning only as these events affect your own life directly. Remember that other people are merely bit-part players in your life drama.

4. List reasons why your own needs and desires should come first, last, and in the middle.

5. Develop communication skills that enhance your ability to help other people understand and acknowledge your position as the center of the universe and their own less significant roles. Help others understand that they are like smaller planets orbiting around you and affected by your gravitational force.

# Meditations

Close your eyes and focus on your breathing. Imagine yourself as the center of the known universe. Feel the galaxies, planets, and stars rotating slowly around you. Now see all the people in your life in like fashion, slowly rotating around you. Know that like the cold, lifeless planets in the universe, these people have no real life or purpose of their own but rather exist only to play cameo appearances in the cosmic movie that is your life.

**WARNING:**

**AVOIDING THE FIRST HABIT** may lead directly to feelings of compassion and humility. In the extreme case, you may actually develop a pervasive, deep recognition that everyone around you is *exactly* like you, i.e.; they have the very same hopes, desires, needs, aspirations, and dreams that you do. And further, their desires and needs are just as valid and meaningful as your own. Exactly as important. They all face the same anxieties, problems, and struggles that you do. All the world is a stage, but the stage has only major actors, title characters; there are no bit actors or cameo roles. No one person's individual drama is any more valid than anyone else's, except perhaps in the mind of that person.

Avoiding the trap of thinking you are the center of the known universe involves, first of all, an understanding and acknowledgement of that very tendency within each of us to want to place ourselves at the center of the universe. Without a full acknowledgement and acceptance of our own tendency to "look out for numero uno", the task of achieving anything close to real humanity is very difficult, if not impossible. Without such an insight into the true depth and power of one's own self-centeredness, the attempt to achieve humility is little more than a frustrating attempt to come across as humble, or worse, an equally self-aggrandizing show of self-debasement to demonstrate the degree of one's humility. Either way, failure.

Someone once wrote that a good definition of true humility was not thinking too highly or too lowly of yourself. I've always liked this definition. For myself, I have certainly spent plenty of time in both extremes of self-assessment. I seem to bounce from the one extreme of heightened self-importance to the other extreme of brutal self-condemnation, rarely pausing long enough to catch my breath in between! Of course most of us would like to think we're humble, but ultimately, we realize there's really no such thing as "tremendous humility", and the more one tries to demonstrate humility, the further one moves away from the target. Our best hope may lie in recognizing the silliness of the little games we play to feed our narcissism by putting on great displays of humility so everyone can admire how humble we are! Self-debasement for show can be just as steeped in self-aggrandizement as the most blatant displays of narcissistic boasting. In truth, I'm no better, but also no worse, than anyone else. And the same is true for you and everyone living on the planet today. No one is any higher or lower than anyone else is, we're just packaged a bit differently. As I once heard someone remark, "Humility is not thinking less of yourself, but rather thinking of yourself less."

Along these lines, I've always liked a story from Zen Buddhist folk literature. The story tells of a famous tiger held in a zoo where it was the main attraction. People came from near and far to see it. But one day, unfortunately, the tiger died. The folks in charge of the zoo panicked because they knew they couldn't afford to obtain another tiger. They decided to resolve this predicament by hiring a beggar to dress up in a tiger suit and pretend to be the famous tiger. Initially, this proved to be a win-win solution: the crowds came to see the famous tiger, the zoo managers prospered, and the beggar gained free room and board.

One day, however, two zoo-goers were arguing in front of the tiger's cage. One man was sure that the tiger was the fiercest animal in the zoo, while the other man was convinced that the lion in the adjacent cage was surely mightier than the tiger. This quarrel became quite heated. Finally the zookeeper decided to settle the issue by allowing the two beasts to fight, but only after the two men had agreed that they would pay the replacement cost of whichever animal was killed.

The gate between the two cages is opened and immediately the lion jumps into the tiger's cage and begins chasing the tiger around the cage. Of course, the man inside the tiger suit is terrified and gives it his all in trying to evade the lion's pursuit, but eventually the lion jumps on top of him. Pinned down beneath the lion, the man thinks he's doomed to be eaten alive by the lion. But just then, the lion whispers in his ear, "Don't worry. I'm the same as you!"

We all have a natural tendency to focus on other peoples' differences and therefore our own uniqueness, often to the exclusion of recognizing the underlying "sameness" we share as members of the human race. We emphasize those differences that are usually based on external appearances, our "tiger and lion suits," if you will. The resultant uniqueness we feel when we persist in this kind of valuation distances us from those around us. But we connect most closely with others when we focus on our internal sameness. And the sameness is overwhelming, when we examine it closely. Can you really question seriously that any other person doesn't have exactly the same needs, hopes, desires, and longings as you do? As we all do? Sure, the specific details of these desires and hopes may look different on the surface (i.e., some people like Brittany Spears and some don't!), but everyone wants to feel good about themselves, to be loved, to be admired, and to have their needs and wants fulfilled.

Recognizing our own quick tendency to make ourselves the centerpiece of the universe helps us realize the obstacles that prevent us from demonstrating true charity. Loving charity is a fundamental virtue sought by all of the major religions. Each religion may employ different terms and symbols, but they all recognize the human tendency of self-centeredness as one of, and perhaps *the* major, obstacle to true charitable behavior. Someone once shared with me a sure-fire way to generate true feelings of loving charity. It's actually a mental exercise that goes like this: picture in your mind someone whose life circumstances are obviously much more difficult than your own. Next, think about all the reasons your own life is better than the other person's life. Then ask yourself, exactly what specific things did you do to *deserve* the blessings and gifts in your own life. If you are able to initially come up with a few superficial justifications and explanations for the "reasons" why you deserve the particular life circumstances you find yourself in (i.e. "I earned a college degree" or "I was born to a good home" or "I worked hard," etc.) don't stop there. Look deeper. What did you do that caused you to deserve to be born to a good home, in America, at this time in history? What did you specifically do to cause yourself to be born with a strong and healthy body? Charity, as it was explained to me, is the insight and feeling that occurs in that exact moment when you realize there is no adequate answer. Or, said another way, it occurs the moment one can say, "there but for the grace of God, go I." And not simply mean it as an expression of sorrow or sympathy for another's circumstances, but as a genuine, existential, and heartfelt acknowledgement and understanding of this fundamental truth. Like the man in the tiger suit, we have the insight that on the inside, we're just like everyone else, with the same desires, hopes, dreams, needs, etc. It's just that we all look different on the outside. And ultimately none of us "deserve" or "earned" in some way the unique circumstances we found ourselves thrust into when we were plopped down here on the planet Earth!

Avoiding the First Habit not only leads to genuine compassion, but may actually make you feel less alone and more a part of mankind. You might begin to take a genuine interest in the concerns and needs of those around you. You may actually begin to connect with the people around you with a kind of depth previously unknown to you. You may begin to see your own problems in an entirely new light and perspective. Mountains may begin to appear more like the molehills they really are. Because of this you might find yourself sleeping more soundly, and feeling less stressed out. You may even begin to see your life as a great adventure with you playing the role of one of many participants in the human family rather than the title character in some unjust cosmic tragedy. Seeing your unique, equally valid (but not *more* valid) role in the context of this huge universal drama of mankind makes it very difficult to find and wallow in your misery. Instead, you have more the feeling of gratitude for the mere and wondrous opportunity to play a small, but important and unique, role in the huge cosmic drama called life! May you play your role with vigor and flare, but don't take your role too seriously!

# 6

# The Second Habit:
# Concentrate On The Things
# You Can't Control

In the previous chapter we learned how to mentally establish ourselves as the rightful centers of the known universe. But we must not make the mistake of resting on our laurels and imagining that this alone will guarantee us lifelong misery. No, there's much more work to be done. The selfish narcissism of being the center of the universe is just the beginning, although it is, as we have learned, the driving force necessary to motivate and sustain us in the difficult task of developing the other six necessary habits. But remember: all of the misery of the Roman Empire wasn't made in a single day!

After establishing one's central location of importance in the universe, one might feel a bit overwhelmed by the vast number of possibilities, by the seemingly limitless options available in terms of how to spend one's time. It would be easy to become frustrated and confused at this point. But we needn't become discouraged or lose hope. We simply need some direction. The Second Habit will help us in dealing with this very problem.

To begin the Second Habit, let's make a list. Take a blank sheet of paper and divide it into two equal columns. In the first column list all the things that are directly and absolutely under your control. You might list such things as your attitude, your actions, your thoughts, and your desires. You may be able to come up with a few more things, but this pretty much sums up the list for most of us. Not a very long list, is it?

Now, in the second column, list all the things in your life over which you have absolutely no control. You know, such things as your health, the future, the past, all of the actions, feelings and opinions of other people, your boss's mood, the U-joints in your car's suspension, your ex-wife's divorce attorney, President Clinton's judgement regarding Monica Lewinsky, the Bush-Gore election, the outcome of this week's lottery drawing, and so on. This list can go on and on, and is limited only by your powers of observation and imagination. In fact, this list pretty much includes everything in your life, except the few items you listed in the first column.

After you've finished, oh, say twelve to twenty pages listing the things you can't control, you're ready for the next step. First, look carefully at your two lists. It should be painfully obvious to you which list is the most important one. The big list, right? Of course, the list with the largest number of items. It's a no-brainer. Now draw a big X through the items in the first column, i.e. the things over which you have some control. We will not waste any more time on these items, so they may be tossed out and disregarded from this point onward. The key now will be to focus all your energy on the items in the second list, on all those things that are clearly beyond your control. You should now concentrate on and devote your full mental efforts to agonize over ways to control those items, even though it's obvious they are beyond your direct control.

Initially, you may be tempted to deal with those items

from the first list, i.e. your thoughts, desires, attitudes, actions, etc. When such temptations occur to you, you must resist at all costs! Working on such aspects of your life is very risky for a number of reasons. For starters, since these things are under your direct control, addressing them head on carries with it the possibility of having to do real work on yourself. And we're talking hard work, often emotionally painful work. Such work may even require some self-discipline; or possibly even...dare I say it...self-control. To make matters worse, dealing with such things carries with it the possibility of assuming responsibility. You see, if something is really within your control, it doesn't take a great leap of faith to come to the conclusion that the responsibility of dealing with it rests solely on your own shoulders. You must assume sole responsibility. Your failure or success in dealing with such things falls directly on no one else but you. This is a most precarious and vulnerable position to place yourself in. Such responsibility opens a whole, ugly can of worms, one that most of us would rather avoid opening.

By now, it should be obvious that dealing with those things that are under our direct control is both risky and potentially painful. Not to mention the fact that such activity wastes valuable time we could and should be using to deal with all those other things that are outside our direct control! These are the things that truly deserve our time and attention. Our lives demand that we address all the situations and aspects of our lives that don't react to or respond to personal our needs. Fortunately, addressing these issues frees us from any risk of having to shoulder the burden of their consequences. This allows us to freely engage in one of life's great pleasures: *having a good B.M.*! Now I'm not talking here about regularity in digestive function, but rather use *BM* to signify a "Bitching/Moaning" session.

You see, all of the things that are outside of our control are a great source of worry and believe me, no amount of time can be truly sufficient to adequately deal with the vast number of things that piss us off. (Remember how you felt the moment the O.J. Simpson jury decision was announced?) All that is required is that we consistently take the time to look around for these things. For this reason, crucial to the Second Habit is this: paying close attention to all the things in our day-to-day lives that are outside of our control. We should practice focusing all of our attention on everything, and I mean *everything*, that doesn't go exactly the way we would like it to go. We'll have a chance to work on this very skill in the exercises later on in this chapter.

Once we've developed the attention skills necessary to quickly identify all the myriad aspects of our lives that do not conform to our exact wants and perceived needs, the next step is correctly handling these things in our minds. What kind of thoughts, do you suppose, should occur to us after recognizing something that has gone contrary to the way we had hoped it would go? Let's say, for example, that your significant other doesn't respond to your need for attention or affection. Your immediate reaction should be to form resentment. Try to imagine any and all possible reasons why this other person might have failed to respond to you in the way you had hoped and expected. Dwell on these reasons. It's known as *ruminating*. Look into it! As you ruminate, you will begin to feel your resentments grow and grow. These feelings of resentment will provide additional motivation and fuel for the next step in the process, which is discussed below. The key point here, however, is that the more resentment and anger you can generate, the more effective your resolve to carry out the Second Habit. Generating resentments is a major part of the Sixth Habit, so we'll come back to this topic in Chapter Ten.

The next step in developing the Second Habit is to figure out ways to change the situation or thing in question. In our example above, this would involve thinking of ways in which we might influence the behaviors of our significant others to make them conform more to our needs and desires. This skill is often referred to as *manipulation*, and manipulation skills are a key part of the Second Habit. By employing manipulation skills, we attempt to get people to respond to us in ways that fulfill our own needs, usually to the exclusion of their own needs and desires. Some of the best tactics involve creating guilt in the minds of other people should they choose behaviors that do not respond to our own needs. Shame, retribution, revenge, martyrdom, deceit, and duplicity are also useful manipulation tactics. Any tactic, however, is useful if it serves to change the thoughts, feelings, or behavior of the people around us in such a manner that they conform more to our particular desires. Our goal is to do everything in our power to manipulate other people to conform to our perception of both who and how they should be.

So there you have it, the Second Habit in a nutshell. Again, the steps are:

1. *Recognize and identify the people, places, and things that aren't directly under our control,*

2. *Develop resentments and frustrations by focusing our thoughts on the incongruency of these things vis-a-vis our wishes and desires, and*

3. *Employ manipulative tactics to change things to match our own particular and specific needs.*

Although hard to believe at first glance, it's really just that simple.

While we're on this step, let's take a moment to discuss a related concept here, namely categorizing and labeling. We've just seen the usefulness of making a list of the things we can control and another list of the things we seem to have no control over. Labeling things and putting them into categories is actually an extremely valuable tool for people who seek to live highly miserable lives. Categorizing things into groups helps us to avoid seeing the uniqueness of particulars by throwing them into broad, generalized categories of universals. This turns out to be a much more efficient way of dealing with the myriad of things we come into contact with in our lives. You see, recognizing and acknowledging the rich diversity in the world is confusing and may even challenge some of our best preconceived ideas. Such confusion takes valuable time away from our chief focus of being the center of the known universe (the First Habit).

A few examples may shed some light on the value of labeling. Remember; labeling works best when you choose the most generalized and broad categories. For example, it's more effective to use the label "women" than the more confining and restrictive term "those women I've dated previously who discovered the truth that my life was a disaster and that I'm a cheat and a liar." In the same way, the label "those crazy fanatics in that there Balkan area of the world" is a more useful concept than "Slovadon Milosevic". Well, you get the idea. We'll talk more about the power of labeling and generalizing in subsequent chapters.

Below are some exercises to help you work on the Second Habit.

## Daily Affirmations

1. Today I will focus on only those things that are completely beyond my direct control.

2. Today I will refuse to be forced into dealing with my own issues or anything over which I have control.

# Exercises

1. Put a check mark next to *only* those items below over which you have no control.

\_\_\_      your family members

\_\_\_      the decision to move far away from your family

\_\_\_      Allan Greenspan

\_\_\_      what stocks to invest in

\_\_\_      your neighbor's dog's behavior

\_\_\_      The decision to pull the trigger when you see the neighbor's dog cleanly in the sights of your 7mm rifle

\_\_\_      whether you will live to see tomorrow

\_\_\_      whether your mother-in-law will live to see tomorrow

\_\_\_      your attitude at work

\_\_\_      your boss' attitude about your attitude at work

2. Pay particular attention in the next hour and list 60 items (people, places, and things) that you would like to change but over which you have no control.

# Meditation

Place yourself in a comfortable position and breath slowly (but not so slowly that you begin to feel dizzy, lightheaded, or think you're Kaiser Wilhelm). Now, for each item in Exercise #2 above, meditate on ideal, imaginary scenarios in which you're able to manipulate those people, places, or things into conforming to how you'd like them to be and act.

## WARNING:

AVOIDING THE SECOND HABIT leads to acceptance and peace of mind. Learning to avoid the Second Habit involves first that we recognize how often we tend to worry about and fret over the things we really have absolutely no control over. Think about how often you get all worked up over such things. As if, somehow, getting all bent out of shape might change the reality of a given situation. Consider for a moment how much of your time and mental energy is wasted in concerning yourself with things outside your control. When you stop and think about it, it's really quite shocking! I know most of the things in my life that tend to get me all out of my gourd have to do with situations where other people don't respond or behave in the way I want them to. Or situations in which inanimate objects, like the carburetor in my car, don't respond the way I want them to! How dare these inanimate objects be so impudent and unresponsive to my needs! I'm somewhat ashamed to recall a fairly recent occasion when my wife caught me in the garage beating on a disobedient and obstinate plumbing valve with a hammer! And, I'm embarrassed to admit, I was pounding on that valve in a punitive manner! Boy, was I going to teach that metal valve a lesson it would not soon forget! That valve was going to think twice before getting stuck on me again, I'll tell you that much! (I can now report that that beating had absolutely no effect on making that valve loosen its grip on that occasion, or on making it more cooperative in any future dealings with it to this day!)

Avoiding the Second Habit involves focusing our attention and energy instead on only those things we can directly control. The good news is that those things are relatively few in number. This takes some of the pressure off our task! What do we really, after all, have control over? Our thoughts, our beliefs, our actions, our responses, and maybe, if we're not married, the way we put the toilet paper on the roller. That's about it folks! Getting caught up in all the other issues outside our control is really nothing more than useless mind games and manipulation! We can exert a lot of time and energy trying to get that other person to behave like we want, but ultimately, it's beyond our direct control. There are, of course, people who do respond to our needs rather than their own. Can you spell co-dependent? But even in these cases such people choose to be co-dependent of their own free will. They always have the power to begin to base their decisions on their own needs. I know all about this because I've been the *co-dependent* in many relationships earlier in my life. I finally recognized this when I had a near death experience, and my girlfriend's life flashed before my eyes! This was a real eye-opener, believe me!

With regard to choices, it's a simple fact that when we base our sense of peace and happiness on the things we have no control over, we place ourselves in extremely shaky and precarious circumstances. Often we do this precisely because we don't want to take any of the responsibility for our own well being, preferring instead to have someone or something to blame for why we don't feel so good about our lives. Basing our sense of self on something outside our direct control is ridiculous because we are essentially giving our power and our freedom over to something outside ourselves. If I decide that I'm only happy when the NASDAQ composite index is above 4000, then I've simply surrendered control over to something outside my control, something that we all know is controlled solely by Allan Greenspan and his pack of cronies! How silly is it to base my sense of contentedness on some aging bureaucrat and his co-conspirators whom I've never met in person but only verbally abused in the safety of my living room?

How much better to base our peace of mind on the things we can control. In this way we become directly responsible for our own happiness and sense of well being. In addition, we retain the power to determine our state of mind in most situations (except, of course, when we discover, with horror, that our spouse has put the toilet paper roll on the wrong way!) The first step, however, is to really recognize our quick tendency to practice the Second Habit, and to catch ourselves getting bent out of shape because of things that, when we really look at them, are completely beyond our control. Following this recognition, we can take a step backward, re-focus on the things we can control, and reorient ourselves. Someone once summarized the key to avoiding the Second Habit this way:

May we all be successful in avoiding the Second Habit and learn to avoid mentally picking up the things that just don't have our names on them!

# 7

# The Third Habit:
# Accumulate and Covet Really Nice Stuff

The first two habits dealt mostly with altering our thinking patterns, namely, thinking our way to the center of the universe and learning to focus on the things beyond our control. The Third Habit, while requiring some mental exertion, goes a step further and actually requires some physical exertion as well. Yes, this habit, unfortunately, will actually require you to get up off the couch (a favorite location to wallow in one's misery, it's true!) and actually do something. Fortunately, however, this physical exertion may be minimized thanks to the modern miracle known as "on-line shopping".

Depending on how one looks at the Third Habit, it can look either exceedingly simple or exceedingly difficult. For this reason we're going to examine this one in steps. As you progress, you'll see that there are unlimited resources in American culture designed expressly to aid you in making this habit a fundamental part of your life.

The first step in cultivating the Third Habit is to develop a deep, unshakable faith in a simple principle (and once again, this could be easily placed on a bumper sticker for those who are so inclined):

*YOUR COMPLETE ESSENCE AND TOTAL VALUE AS A PERSON IS EQUAL TO THE SUM OF THE STUFF YOU OWN.*

Sounds pretty simple, right? The real key to this Third Habit, however, is to believe this principle completely, unquestionably, unwaveringly, and whole-heartedly. You might mistakenly think, "OK, I'll admit that the things I own do, in fact, help to express who I am, but I possess some value beyond my possessions, right?" Wrong! Such weak-minded belief will simply not do. To really become miserable, you must believe beyond a shadow of a doubt that all of your value as a person stems entirely from the things you own. In other words, you have *no* value outside of your material possessions. Your possessions completely determine who you are and exactly what your value as a person is. Period. End of discussion. Anyone who desires to know your value as a human being need look no further than the house you live in, the car you drive, the clothes you wear, the size of your stock portfolio, and so on and so forth. Simple accounting.

Now, at this point you may be offended by the apparent emphasis on materialism and you may say, "Hey, I refuse to put so much emphasis on money (or filthy lucre)! The Bible says that love of money is the root of all evil, don't you know?" (In actuality, George Bernard Shaw more correctly pointed out, however, that it was *lack of money* that was the true root of evil!) To this objection, let me respond by saying that I'm not suggesting a total emphasis on monetary things. Money, after all, is just currency. A means of trade and commerce. It would be ludicrous to put a large emphasis on money alone. What I'm talking about here is not money, but rather "stuff". We all can relate to "stuff" and it's stuff that should define our value and worth as people. And the nicer and the more stuff you have, the more value you have.

One of the beauties of this system is its sheer simplicity. You see, everyone wants to be "OK," to be accepted by others and viewed as being "fine." So what could be more simple than to have your "OK-ness" as a person be something that you could purchase and display for all to see? Such a value system would save you an inordinate amount of time since you wouldn't need to spend time interacting with other individuals to get to know them inside. Rather, you simply display who you are by flaunting your "stuff" and, just as simply, you can look at other people's possessions to understand who they are. And saving time in this way frees up more time for working more hours to make more money to buy more stuff to further add to one's worth as a person. Easy, eh?

Another point that should be made about this possessive attitude is that it can extend beyond just stuff to include our relationships with other people. We can learn to think of our family, friends, business associates, etc., as possessions. In this way, the people in our lives "add" value to us in a way that any accountant would easily understand. And, fortunately, the language of our culture facilitates this type of mindset: "I *have* a wife and four children", "This is *my* friend" and "I *have* many friends." As Erich Fromm pointed out in his book *To Have Or To Be*, even our modern cultural language encourages us to think using possession-oriented syntax.

Which brings up another idea we should discuss, namely work. One can easily see how work fits within this value system. Why is work important? It should be obvious to you. Work is important because it's the means by which a person gets the money to obtain the possessions that subsequently determine that person's self-worth. And how, then, should one value one's work? Of course, we'd all like to work doing something we enjoy and feel good about doing. You know, work that makes us feel that we are making a contribution to better our community and the world at large. But if this becomes the purpose and focus of one's work, then one loses sight of the real point of work: *to make money*. Hence, the value of any given job is directly proportional to how much it pays. Once again, we see the profound simplicity of this value system. A person does not need to waste his or her time pondering one's talents, the nature of a given career, etc. No, one needs only look at the bottom line, i.e. the number on IRS form W-2: gross tips, wages, salary. This simplifies the task of finding a career because each job can be evaluated and compared to other jobs based on the bottom line.

Such a mindset also makes it easier to compare the value of your job to that of another person. Simply compare salaries and there you have it. Let's consider a simple example. Which job has more value, being a professional basketball player who makes $12 million a year or being a grade school teacher who makes $35,000 a year? See how simple it is? Of course, the answer is the professional basketball player. But is it really always this easy to compare the relative values of two professions or careers? Of course not. Often, for example, a person may be trying to compare two careers with nearly identical salaries and it becomes difficult to determine which job is the best. In a case like this, one must go a bit further and compare each job's pension plan, medical and dental benefits, profit-sharing plan, stock options, etc. By taking these extra steps, even in such comparisons, a person should be able to attach a dollar figure to each of these benefits and determine the most valuable job accurately and subsequently head down the best career path.

Once you've found the highest paying job possible, you can then begin to establish your self-identity and value as a person. All you've got to do now is begin to accumulate all kinds of "stuff". At first it may be difficult to know exactly what to buy. We've all experienced this dilemma. This is how every novice capitalist feels at first. It's natural to feel this way, especially in light of the dizzying array and vast assortment of "stuff" out there. To help with this dilemma, then, let me offer a few general guidelines to help you become a good consumer with a healthy self-concept:

*Rely on the advertising media* to help you decide what it is that you must have in order to truly "be somebody." Toward this end, those friendly folks in the marketing industry are more than willing to help you, whether it be through TV commercials, magazine ads, Internet banners, or whatever. In fact, their whole purpose and reason for existence is to help you decide exactly what you need in order to express who you are. Pay particular attention to the people in the ads; if the person looks like the kind of person you want to be, simply make it a goal to get all the stuff that the person in the ad is obviously enjoying and using to be the kind of person he or she is trying to be. Got it? It's really quite simple when you stop and think about it.

*Closely observe the purchases of your friends, neighbors, co-workers*, essentially everyone around you, to discover purchasing hints to add value to your life. People are often totally ignorant of just how much they wanted or needed a particular possession until a friend or neighbor buys one and reminds them of their hidden need. This is the so-called "Keeping Up With The Jones" principle. It's an important concept to help you become an informed consumer.

*Respond to uncomfortable feelings you might have by making an appropriate purchase.* For example, let's say you're feeling unhappy or inadequate. Ask yourself why you're feeling this way and then ponder deeply what you might buy to make this uncomfortable feeling go away. As you come to understand yourself better, you'll get better and better at quickly identifying the most effective purchase to, as they say, "chase those old blues away."

*Remember: there just ain't no feeling so bad or unpleasant that it can't be chased away by buying the right stuff!*

So, as you can see, the Third Habit is really quite simple. American culture and the advertising industry reinforce it at every point in our lives. It is a habit that is literally pounded into our heads on a daily basis from the moment we were old enough to turn our heads in the direction of the TV set! Nevertheless, below are a few exercises to help solidify the "Covet Really Nice Stuff Habit":

## Daily Affirmations

1. Dress like the man (woman), be the man (woman).

2. I am what I own.

3. I am what I have.

4. I am not a human *being*. I am a human *having*.

## Exercises

1. List three personal characteristics that you would like people to think you have. Then for each characteristic, list three items you could purchase which would help convince other people that you actually had these qualities or personal characteristics

2. Pick up any recent magazine. Flip through the pages for ten minutes, looking only at the ads. Then list 20 items that you currently don't have, but that, if you had them, would greatly add to your general sense of well being and security.

# Meditations

Imagine someone who is a better, more self-actualized individual than you (hint: it could be anyone who makes $20,000 more per year than you do). Now, meditate and use imagery to see yourself as this other person. Literally place yourself in this person's shoes...and clothes...and car...and house...and relationships. Imagine how much better you'd feel about yourself as a unique individual if only you made a bit more money or had the same kind and amount of stuff that this other person has. Stop the meditation immediately if you begin to entertain serious thoughts about killing this other person.

**WARNING:**

**AVOIDING THE THIRD HABIT** leads to becoming a human *being* instead of just a human *having*. Like the other Habits, the first step is to recognize our own tendency to place our sense of self-worth in our possessions. Sometimes we become so steeped in our possession-oriented culture that we don't even recognize how much we identify ourselves with our possessions. None of us, (with the exception of that one Vietnamese guy who does the real estate infomercials about how he became a multimillionaire!), would dare admit that we base our whole sense of self on our material or nonmaterial possessions, but consider this. Think of the last time that you were asked to introduce yourself to a group of strangers. How many of us responded by saying something like, "Well, *my* name (I own it!) is Tony, and I *have* a wife and four kids. I *have* a job at McDonald's. I *have* a doublewide mobile home. I *have* a Dachshund who had to have his testicles removed and replaced with brass balls and we named him Sparkey." Except for the human-interest part about Sparkey's medical history, notice that such an introduction is all about possession, nothing about the essence of who we are.

Try the exercise yourself by answering the question, "Who are you?" Then try to do it without using any possessive verbs or possessive pronouns. It's quite difficult, isn't it? And why is this? Why is it so hard for most of us to describe ourselves without some reference to our possessions? I think a lot of this has to do with our possession-oriented culture. I think most of us grew up in a society that more or less told us that we *are* what we *own*. And I think most of us believed it. And continue to believe it.

Recognizing our strong tendency to identify our "selves" with our possessions is just the first step in avoiding the Third Habit of miserable living. The next step is to find a good reason to give up our reliance on this emphasis. It's not sufficient to conjure up all kinds of morally- or religiously based commandments against the evils of materialism. This approach might evoke guilt about having lots of stuff, but most of us would continue to secretly base our sense of well being on our possessions. If we set aside our moral and religious knee-jerk reactive negativity toward materialism, is there a better reason to not place our faith in our material "stuff"? Why should we not base our value as a person on our possessions? So how, then, can we escape our reliance on possessions as a means of self-realization?

When we ponder this question thoroughly, the answer becomes fairly simple: it's because none of our possessions comes with a full lifetime guarantee! (with the exception of this book, of course!) None of our possessions (including our relationships) are guaranteed for any length of time at all, let alone a lifetime. Think about it for a moment. Name one possession that you think you own that you know will be yours for the length of your life, *guaranteed*. It's impossible. Everything we think we own could be taken away from us at any minute. If you don't really believe this as an indisputable fact, consider the people living their lives in 1945 in Hiroshima.

Regardless of all the legal documents, paper guarantees, and the FDIC sticker on the door of your local bank, everything you think you own is an illusion. It's nothing more than a mind game. It might come as a shock to Charleston Heston, but in truth even his beloved rifle *will* be one day pried from his cold, dead fingers and it won't belong to him any more!

And so, when we base our sense of self and peace of mind on the security of our possessions, in truth we are placing our security in a very insecure place. Add to this the fact that our material possessions (excluding wine and Barbie dolls kept in the original packaging!) are constantly depreciating in value. If you don't believe this concept, picture in your mind a 1977 El Camino. You remember those fashionable car-like trucks or truck-like cars? Well, consider that in 1977 there were actually people, who coveted, I mean really coveted, one of those things! What do you think one of those things is worth today (assuming you could actually find one that still runs)?

And thus, when we place our sense of personal value in material things, we give our power over to the possessions and in a very real sense, we become slaves to them. We reduce our freedom when we directly link it to our possessions. Goethe once remarked that there are no chains so powerful as the ones the captives can't see, and this is certainly true with regard to the strength of the chains we forge to attach ourselves to our possessions. There is a story of a Western journalist traveling in India who was taken to visit a holy man. This particular holy man had lived a hermit's existence, living alone in a high mountain cave for thirty or forty years. His only possession was a simple clay bowl that he used to beg for rice once a week when he went down into the village. Upon entering the cave, the journalist stumbled on a rock and fell on the old man's clay bowl, breaking it to bits. Before the journalist could apologize for destroying this man's only earthly possession, the old man shouted out, "Free at last! Free at last!"

Most of us are familiar with the difficulty that Native Americans had in understanding the white man's concept of land ownership. To the Native Americans, the idea that a person could actually own something like land was preposterous. This fact had much more to do with the Dutch settlers purchasing Manhattan for $24 than the savvy Donald Trump-like business tactics of the Dutch! In the minds of the Native American inhabitants of Manhattan, they had really pulled a fast one on these ignorant white men, something akin to selling the Brooklyn Bridge to an unsuspecting tourist. They had received $24 for something that, to their mindset, couldn't be owned any more than someone could own the sky or the wind. (But, of course, they had never met a corporate attorney before!) But they actually had the *right* idea. In fact, the real illusory nature of ownership doesn't just apply to land, but extends to all possessions. If you think you really own something, just stop making the payments on it and you'll discover the illusions of ownership faster than the repo man can bust into your car!

One exercise to help overcome one's tendency toward material attachment is this: take any possession you think you own or an item you just gotta have to "be somebody." Visualize that object in your mind in all it's radiant, self-actualizing splendor! Next, picture that same object twenty years from now sitting on a table in someone's driveway garage sale! See in your mind the "$2 or best offer" tag attached to it. See a middle-aged man with a large beer gut pick up your item and say, "What a piece of junk!" Consider this fact literally: everything in your life that you value so heavily now, will one day be that $2 or $5 item in someone's garage sale! So why do we place our sense of self-satisfaction in all this junk anyway?

In reality, the only things we own are our memories, our thoughts, our choices, and our actions. And so, when we realize that we can't really own anything material anyway, why would we be so deluded or foolish, then, to base our sense of well being on something so unreliable, so untrustworthy, as our possessions? We shouldn't.

As a final note before leaving the subject of the total futility of trying to base our personal happiness and sense of self-worth on our material possessions, I'd like to share a personal anecdote, one that has taught me in a very real way how foolish it is to place one's security in on one's material assets. A local physician I am aware of (I'll call him Dr. L. Les Worth, not his real name, of course!) had more than taken advantage of the Medicare system and had thus, prior to retiring, amassed wealth in the neighborhood of $15 million! (And some people wonder why the Medicare system is experiencing fiscal difficulties now!) Following his retirement, I have had the opportunity to watch this man continue to pursue every possible angle, however shameful, in his unending quest to obtain more wealth. Many of these greedy schemes have cost him the respect of his peers, both in the medical profession and the general community. He has actually placed his pursuit of wealth above many of his lifelong friendships, allowing them to fall by the wayside. And still his pursuit of wealth goes on. It is as if his very soul were inextricably tied to his possessions. It is very sad and tragic to see this shadow of a man, growing old alone, living out a shallow existence that no amount of material wealth could possibly save. It's painful to observe such a pathetic example of materialism at its extreme.

Why is the futility of trying to gain happiness and peace of mind through the pursuit of material gains always so clear to outsiders yet so difficult for us to see in ourselves? So let's just all stop being so silly and end the insane accumulation of all this stuff, OK?

# 8

# The Fourth Habit:
# Focus On Fear

In the last chapter we learned the importance of accumulating material items. This next habit, the Fourth Habit (for those keeping count), follows very naturally after the Third Habit. This habit encourages us to focus on fear and fear follows accumulation of possessions like Michael Jackson follows young boys, believe me.

One of the great paradoxes of life is this: we feel insecure about ourselves and this sense of inadequacy instills great fear in us. Fear leads to anxiety, anxiety leads to desperation, and desperation leads to a frantic need to do something, anything, to escape these uncomfortable feelings. As we learned in the last chapter, the media (advertising) is ever ready to help us solve this dilemma by providing us with the obvious solution: *buy stuff!* What a relief when we discover there is an easy way to make this nagging sense of insecurity go away and that it is only as far away as the nearest mall...oops...only as far away as our computers and the internet. "A purchase or two a day keeps the insecurity away" has become our anthem. The great paradox, however, is that inextricably linked to each material possession is the fear of losing that very same possession. And the more valuable the particular thing is, the greater the accompanying fear. It's a perfect example of a vicious cycle!

The more you live in fear of insecurity, the greater your need to obtain material possessions to escape this fear, but the more material possessions you accumulate, the greater becomes your fear of losing these very possessions. And the greater the sense of fear of losing material possessions is, the more one feels the need to obtain more possessions to rid oneself of that fear. A never-ending cycle spiraling into ever greater levels of misery and credit card debt!

But our goal is to achieve misery quickly and efficiently, so what, we might ask ourselves, stands in our way of achieving this goal? Exactly! Anything that diverts us from or makes us forget about our fear. Hence the Fourth Habit, Focus On the Fear! This is not as easy as it might seem at first glance. First of all, we must remember that we live in a culture that encourages distraction, as we mentioned earlier. Any kind of mindless entertainment, be it a movie devoid of plot but heavy on sex and violence or an equally mindless video game, will divert us from awareness of our fears, if only temporarily. For this reason, it's important that we make an effort, a real concentrated daily effort to dwell on all those things we fear. And again, as with all the other Seven Habits, this one becomes easier with repetition and practice.

And so, we need to learn to focus attention on our fears. And the first step is defining exactly what those particular fears are. One of the biggest and best fears that most of us have, as mentioned above, is the fear of losing our material things. Now, some of readers may say at this point, "But wait a minute! I don't really have much in the way of material things, so I don't have much fear in this regard." But I would respond by telling you that the answer is simple. A great deal of fear, an infinite amount, actually, can be generated simply by fearing that you will never get the things you don't currently have! And remember that for us all, the income level, at which we "have arrived" and are considered financially secure, is always

10 to 30% greater than whatever income we currently have. A lot of fear can be generated simply by dwelling on the belief that you will never quite make it to that higher level of income. And somehow we just know in our heart of hearts that total financial security and peace of mind would befall us like manna from heaven, if only that level of income could be obtained! See how simple this can be?

Besides the loss of and the inaccessibility of material possessions, what other fears can be tapped into in order to increase our overall level of fear-awareness? Here are a few suggestions:

*Paranoid delusions: consider that other people are probably to be talking negatively about you. These people are probably not just engaged in idle chatter, but almost certainly are laying out elaborate plots to cause your ultimate downfall in the most humiliating, public, and shameful manner possible.*

*Natural disasters: these are a great source of fears and are readily available in the daily newspapers and TV news reports. Hurricanes, flooding, earthquakes, Allan Greenspan speeches, and other unpredictable "acts of God" are great focal points on which to center our worrying. And remember, that although commonly thought of as "senseless acts of God", you can also foster additional fear by considering that maybe the natural disaster that strikes you tomorrow is actually being directed by God expressly for the purpose of screwing up your life! Such thinking patterns will allow you to live in fear of "the big hurricane" even if you live in Iowa.*

*Unlikely future events: besides the natural disasters mentioned above, this category would include such things as the fear of not winning next Wednesday's lottery, fear of not getting a response to the romantic e-mail you sent to Cindy Crawford or Brad Pitt, fear of deer fly tick bites and dying of Lyme Disease, fear of dealing with worldwide celebrity, fear of acquiring AIDS from a public toilet seat, etc., etc. As you can see, this is a wide open area and the fears are limited only by one's imagination since the source of these don't even have to be possible based on the best evidence of scientific reason or common sense.*

*Political events: another good source of fears which don't even need to be based on any sense of good judgement or common sense. For example, the fear that if gun control laws are enacted, an Orwellian nightmare of total federally policed corruption will ensue within, oh, say nine months or so (think NRA!). Or the fear that if homosexual marriages are publicly sanctioned, we will all be brainwashed to give in to our latent homosexual tendencies and gay people will take over all aspects of control and actually force us all to have homosexual experiences against our will! Or the fear of all those other "evil" nations that are just waiting for their chance to invade our country, take it over, and subject our citizens to abject slavery (why else would we have multi-billion dollar defense budgets, after all?)*

*Religion: in our search for specific things to fear, this category, religion, is hard to beat. It's been a favorite source of fear for millennia and continues to be a great focus for fear. Fear of God's punishment for breaking His commandments, fear of not knowing what His commandments are, fear of not achieving a "mansion in heaven" with enough square footage or a good floor plan for entertaining, fear of having the wrong religion or being in the wrong sect within the correct religion, the list goes on and on. Even the fear that God does not exist at all and subsequently having all of one's righteous efforts come to naught are excellent additional sources of fear and anxiety.*

*Expectations of other people: another great source of fear, one limited only by your ability to imagine and exaggerate in your mind all the various and conflicting expectations that other people have of who you should be and what you should be doing with your life. Most people in your life would be more than happy to share their expectations with you with little or no prompting. Once you know what these expectations are, it's simply a matter of concentrating on your inevitable inadequacy in fulfilling these expectations and viola!, huge amounts of fear can be created effortlessly. Fortunately, few people can even come close to fulfilling all these expectations because inevitably many of them will conflict with one another, making it essentially impossible to fulfill them all.*

Of course, there are many more sources of fear than we could possibly discuss in this short chapter. The great thing is, it doesn't matter whether these fears are justified by the reality of your present or future situation or not. Generating fear does not require any particular real conditions in your life. One needs only to conjure up the fear in one's mind. Imagination is actually the best means of creating the largest amounts of fear. For example, let's say that everything is going well at work in your office. Sales are up, employees are happy, your supervisor is pleased with your work. Nothing to fear, right? Wrong! Just imagine some random catastrophic event, i.e. the building being blown up by terrorists or the company going bankrupt because of a frivolous lawsuit, and kaboom! Suddenly, the whole situation changes and work becomes a huge source of worry and fear. Just about any situation can be easily turned into a great source of stress and fear simply by imagining potential adverse situations that might come to pass and then focusing on them as being likely to happen. It's really that simple!

Below are a few exercises to help us increase the levels of fear in our lives:

## Daily Affirmations

1. I will live in constant fear of the unknown, the unlikely, and the implausible.

2. To know you is to fear you.

3. To not know you is to fear you.

## Exercises

1. List the three most secure things in your life right now. Then write down for each item two possible, although unlikely events that would quickly shatter the security of each.

a. _____

b. _____

c. _____

2. For each of the seemingly harmless items listed below, write down how each item might actually be a thing to be greatly feared. For example, if the item were a harmless housefly, you might imagine that it was actually a vector for some kind of fatal, as-yet-undiscovered, virus.

a.) Teddy bear_____

b.) Grandma_____

c.) A refund check from the IRS_____

d.) A comfy lounge recliner_____

e.) A loved one_____

f.) A piece of fresh-baked apple pie_____

g.) A puppy_____

3. Think of and list 10 things that could happen tomorrow that would utterly destroy your reputation and life as you now know it. Then do the same thing but this time list 10 things that might happen tomorrow which would result in your immediate death.

## Meditations

1. Assign one item from Exercise #2 above to each night of the week. Then spend 10 to 15 minutes that night meditating on that item. Sit in a comfortable position (but not in a terrifying comfy lounge recliner!). Close your eyes lightly. First imagine in your mind the selected item in its harmless state. Then imagine you see the item change into the object of fear. Then, imagine and visualize that item causing your ultimate demise. Lastly, bring yourself slowly back to the reality of the present moment but retain a lingering memory of that item such that, should you come into contact with that item in your daily life, you would instantly shout out, "*Away from me, you cursed object of Lucifer!*"

2. Close your eyes and imagine someone in your life whom you trust implicitly, someone beyond reproach, and someone with whom you'd trust your very life. See that person in your mind, smiling sincerely at you. Now imagine that that same smile becomes more sarcastic, eventually changing into a smirk. Now imagine that that person actually has been fooling you all this time and that he or she actually is plotting your destruction. Continue in this manner until you have concocted in your mind all the necessary and sufficient reasons why that may actually be the case. Do this meditation with a different person in mind each night until there is no one left in your previous circle of friends whom you could trust. Then begin the process again with each person to keep your fears of these persons fresh and alive in your mind.

3. Before going to bed, pick one story of a catastrophic event out of the newspaper. Close your eyes and visualize that same event happening in your neighborhood with the very epicenter of the calamity being your home. In addition to the natural disaster you've conjured up in your imagination, imagine that somehow you are, plausibly, being blamed for that disaster. Now imagine your neighbors and former friends, torches in hand, carrying you off with the intent of bringing about your ultimate demise.

4. Close your eyes. Imagine yourself getting the morning newspaper, only to find that the cover story is a complete exposé on all the stupid, shameful and embarrassing things you've done in your life, including a few that you don't immediately recall. Focus your mind on your feelings of shame and then imagine in your mind that your local newspaper is at this very moment printing that story as tomorrow's cover story.

## WARNING:

**AVOIDING THE THIRD HABIT** leads to peace of mind and serenity. It begins by understanding, recognizing, and avoiding our tendency to fall victim to our fears. Fear is, for many of us, the thing that most commonly upsets our peace of mind. Think about how much time we spend each day engulfed in ideas involving fear? Many of us are probably so habituated to thinking about the future and worrying about all the possible outcomes of future scenarios that to do otherwise would feel totally foreign to us. Often we rationalize this mental activity of worrying about the future by labeling it as "planning for the future." We tell ourselves that thinking about future events is a necessary way of preparing ourselves for it. But the fact is, most often we are really just indulging ourselves in our fears and this instantly causes the loss of any peace of mind we might otherwise have.

A wise person once said that there are only two qualities one needs to have in order to be happy. The first of these is *generosity*, which comes in large part by avoiding the First and Second Habits, and the second is *courage*. Often, when we think of courage, we imagine heroic acts of bravery and the like. But courage here refers to a mental activity of recognizing the illusory nature of our fears and refusing to allow them to disturb our peace of mind.

Part of the problem for many of us is that we have developed a mind set that naturally assumes that the things that cause us to feel fear must be real and dangerous threats to our well-being. It becomes a mental reflex: we feel fear...we assume direct threat to our lives...we panic or feel deep anxiety. Why is this?

To understand this, we need to go back to our days long ago when we human creatures lived in the midst of real and imminent danger. Our early ancestors lived in constant fear of being sprung upon by a huge beast with large nasty teeth and instantly torn apart and eaten alive. (i.e. by a saber-toothed tiger!) In nature's wisdom, we evolved a survival mechanism in our brains to help improve our chances for survival. This has been called the *fight or flight response* and it is an instinctive behavior that is hard-wired in our brains. Here's how it works. Saber-toothed tiger appears, and the brain sends chemicals to the muscles of the body to ready them for either fight or flight. Prior to the invention of weapons, the fighting route was less adaptive to survival than the flighting route when it came to saber-toothed tigers! It was this situation that led to the first definition of FEAR (= F#*k Everything And Run!). Those who ran (and especially those who ran the fastest!) had the best chance of surviving and passing their genes on to their offspring. This is why there is no such thing as a *fight or negotiate response*. Or a *flight or calmly stop and consider your* *options response.* Or the *fight or you'll hear from my lawyer response.*

Because of the deeply inbred nature of the fight or flight response in our brains, we continue to be controlled by it. The problem is that today, unless you're a pediatric oral surgeon, your chances of being bitten by an irrational, wild beast are quite slim. Despite this, anything that illicits fear causes our brains to release the chemicals that prepare our bodies for fighting or flighting. These chemicals rev up our bodies, make our blood pressure go sky high, and cause us to think and sometimes say things like, "I'm going to get a hammer and just smash this @!#! VCR to smithereens!" or, "If that @!##! waiter ignores us again, let's just get up and get the *#!! out of here!" Sometimes these responses are helpful, sometimes not so helpful. Problem is, these same chemicals are released even in situations of perceived threats, i.e., whenever our minds conjure up imaginary fears. Thus, our bodies and brains get pumped up, but there's often no one to fight or flight from! These chemicals destroy our peace of mind and serenity and make us miserable. Ultimately these chemicals cause us to have migraine headaches, low back pain, ulcers, heart attacks and strokes.

And the problem with perceived threats and the fear that follows them is that they seem to be everywhere, constantly. Or at least they can be, as we saw in the discussion and exercises of the Fourth Habit. It's clear that we can create an unlimited number of fears in our minds and also that we can make these fears appear bigger and more threatening by simply thinking about them. ("Making a mountain out of a mouse turd!" as my Uncle Phineas was fond of saying!) When we focus on any fear, it becomes bigger. This is one of the unbreakable truths of the universe: the things we focus on become larger.* So how, then, do we deal with and overcome these fears? With courage. But how?

Courage begins when we face our fears honestly. This is a radical concept for many of us who may have grown up with the idea that being brave meant facing something fearful, all the while pretending not to be scared. Never let 'em see you sweat (or tremble or shake), as the popular saying tells us. Pretending that we are not afraid or that fear doesn't exist is a sham and a lie, and while it may look good on the surface, only causes our inner experience of fear to increase. To really defuse a fear requires looking directly at it, staring right into the heart of the fear. As the Buddhists like to express it, it means looking deeply into the nature of the thing, in this case, our fears.

When we look deeply into the true nature of our fears, we discover them to be mere mental illusions, without any true substance. A tiger can certainly hurt you, but fear of a tiger that doesn't exist as a real threat can't kill you (at least not directly). Let's say you live in New York City and you've conjured up in your head that a tiger is going to escape from the Brooklyn Zoo, steal subway fare, and make it's way to Manhattan, where you live. You are so certain of this that you live in constant fear and dread that you will certainly fall prey to this tiger one day and be killed. Several years later, you drop dead from a massive heart attack, caused, of course, in large part by the damaging effects of chronic over-stimulation of the fight or flight chemicals in your body. Since this chemical flood was caused by your illogical fear of being killed by an escaped tiger. In a sense, you really do end up being killed by this tiger! Logical, isn't it?

And so it is with the vast majority of the fears we conjure up in our minds. Someone once estimated that a full 99% of the things we worry about never come to pass. Or as someone else

*often does not work when it comes to the male sex organ, however, and focusing on baseball statistics is much more effective!

put it, "the worst things in our lives never occur!" And the 1% of things that do occur, are things that we wouldn't have been able to do anything to avoid anyway, regardless of how revved up our fight or flight responses were. And so, we must logically conclude that 100% of our fears potentially lead to the release of neuro-transmitters from our brains that are of no help to us and actually can cause illness and premature death. Winston Churchill was indeed correct in identifying our fears (and their consequences) as the only things ultimately to be feared.

When we look deeply into the true nature of our fears, we begin to see them as less threatening than they might at first appear. Unacknowledged fear is much like believing there is a ferocious man-eating dragon in the closet, but when we open the closet door (and face our fear), there is just a tiny plastic dragon toy. So it is with our fears. We can chose to sit on the couch and magnify our fear of this thing in the closet. Or we can look in the closet by looking deeply at the true nature of our fears and thereby discover the little plastic toy that was causing such mental torment. The natural response to this discovery is, of course, to laugh. And laughing at our blown-out-of-proportion fears and ourselves is an extremely effective way to increase our peace of mind and happiness!

# 9

# The Fifth Habit:
# Discover the Inner Victim in You!

Once again, let's quickly review our progress along the road to misery. Hopefully you, the reader, are spending a good part of your waking hours practicing the previous steps as part of a diligent program to gain some serious misery. First, we acknowledge ourselves as the center of and focal point of the universe. Each day we focus only on those things over which we have absolutely no control, and we actively avoid those few things over which we do have some degree of control. Next, we fully attach our sense of self-worth on our material possessions and exert our best efforts to accumulate more and more material things. Then we focus on all our fears, both real and imagined, magnifying them in the process. With just these first four habits we are now truly well on the way to an overwhelmingly miserable life. But lest we become distracted from our primary goal, we must keep in mind that there's more work to be done, more habits to learn and practice.

The Fifth Habit is an exercise in discovery. For some of us it involves becoming reacquainted with a part of ourselves from the past that we may have forgotten. For others, this may involve becoming acquainted with a part of ourselves that we have never recognized. Yet, regardless of whether its a new acquaintance or more of a reunion, it involves getting in touch with an aspect of ourselves that each of us holds within. And for any of us who are still in denial regarding this aspect, it can be created easily enough, with a little help from our imagination. You see, I'm referring here of that part of our personality that is constantly being attacked, held back, discriminated and plotted against, chased, hunted down, frustrated at every step, unfairly scrutinized, and mistreated at every turn. It's that part of us that never gets a fair shake, that part that is absolutely convinced that the rules of the game are stacked against us (or that the rules of the game don't even apply to us!). That's right! I'm referring to the inner victim inside us all. The Fifth Habit involves getting in touch with this poor little sh*t!

The first step is to let go of any denial regarding this aspect of your personality and acknowledge the very real existence of this little victim inside us. This is best done by meditation and visual imagery. We'll do some meditation exercises later to visualize our personal victim, but for now the important thing is to acknowledge that we have this little victim inside us, a victim who has been slighted over and over again our entire lifetimes. This victim needs our help to find expression in our lives and it's our job to allow our little victims this opportunity for expression. Take a moment now to acknowledge your own inner victim by saying, "Hello, little victim! Don't be scared, I'm your friend!" Say this in an upbeat and positive way so as not to frighten your victim, who may quite likely be very paranoid and suspicious of your true motives for wanting to make this contact. (Some readers may find it helpful to mark their index finger with a little face but if so, resist the temptation to say things like, "RED RUM!" or "I'm Mr. Freshness and I use Ziploc baggies!" Your victim may misinterpret such antics as direct assaults, shameful teasing, or even blatant persecutions. Not a very healthy way to start off a new relationship of this sort!)

Building a solid relationship is the next goal. This involves staying in tune to the things your little victim self is trying to tell you. Eventually the goal is to listen so closely to your inner victim that it is the voice you hear most clearly of all! Listen especially closely for such things as:

*"Those dirty #@\*## are always out to get me!"*

*"These things always happen to me!"*

*"If only it weren't for (supply your own noun here), everything in my life would be just peachy!"*

As you listen closely to your inner victim, you will find yourself being drawn in as an accomplice, a co-victim, if you will. You and your inner victim will become a well-oiled team, always on the defensive and quick to spot the many, often covert, plots, schemes, and traps laid out for the both of you to sabotage every aspect of your life. You'll begin to see the true devious intentions of all the people and organizations in your life. You'll begin to understand that most of these people's energy and resources are in fact directed toward the sole purpose of destroying any slim chance you might otherwise have had to achieve even a tiny shred of happiness in this life. And these plots will appear even in the actions and behaviors of people and organizations that you might previously have viewed as being well intentioned and harmless.

One of the great things about discovering and befriending your inner victim is that there are many different kinds of victims available to you, each with its own unique way of being a victim. Consequently, you don't have to assume just one stereotypical victim role. Just like picking out what kind of clothes you're going to put on in the morning, you get to chose the kind of victim you're going to be each day! In fact, you and your victim may decide to use different victim styles in different settings during a single day. Have fun with it. Some of the most popular victim styles are:

*The hard-core loud victim-* *this style is characterized by loud expression of one's victimhood to any- and everybody, whenever, wherever, regardless of the situation. Tends to be precipitated or exacerbated by alcoholic beverages.*

*The suffering hero-* *this style takes pleasure in and wants credit for being the victim. Also known as martyrdom.*

*The silent victim-* *this type does not appear to be a victim at all on the outside, but internally is constantly aware of and angered by the clear victimization it must suffer. This style might think, "This #@#\*#@ jerk thinks I'm going to be his slave and all he does is demand things! I'll show this idiot!" but when his mouth opens what comes out is, "Sir, here is your Big Mac. I'm really sorry about the wait. Could I get you some ketchup for your fries?"*

*The "I'm-keeping-track-of-each-incident" victim-* *this type may seem to shrug off apparent offenses but inside keeps accurate and detailed little mental notes documenting each incident in order to "keep score". This provides the ammunition for future retaliatory strikes.*

Of course, there are numerous other styles or styles. In addition, it's possible to employ various combinations of the above styles. The important thing, however, is to be alert to every possible offense and to never, never, under any circumstance, allow even the most innocent (on the surface) episode pass by unnoticed without careful conscious scrutiny of its possible persecutory implications toward you. With enough practice and teamwork with your inner victim, you'll find yourself able in most cases to find an underlying malicious intention in all the previously innocent-appearing situations in your life.

Below you'll find exercises to help get in touch with your inner little victim. Make this the day that you look your little victim in the eye and say, "I think this may be the beginning of a long and sick relationship!"

## Daily Affirmations

1. Good morning, my little victim!

2. Today we'll look out for the many people, places, and things that will certainly try to take advantage of us. And then we'll let them victimize us.

3. We must not be smart enough, or good enough, and dog-gone-it, people must not like us!

## Exercises

1. Reflect for a moment on everything that happened to you during the last week. Now list three events that occurred that were clearly the direct result of the covert plotting of people in your life who live solely for the purpose of seeing your ultimate humiliation and downfall.

a._____

_____

b._____

_____

c._____

_____

2. List the three major reasons that the Supreme Creator of the Universe also wants to see your ultimate humiliation and downfall.

a._____

_____

b._____

_____

c._____

_____

## Meditations

Close your eyes. Make yourself comfortable or at least as comfortable as you are capable of being. Concentrate on your breathing. Now, try to visualize in your mind someone who looks almost exactly like you do, except a whole lot more angry and paranoid. And a bit smaller. And pathetic-looking. You somehow sense that perhaps this is your inner victim. Greet him by saying, "Hello, little victim me, you poor, sorry little sh*t! Don't be scared! I'm your friend, your buddy." Approach your little victim person and begin talking. Begin to discuss the events of the day. As you do, you'll find that your little buddy has been trampled on all day by the many people, places and things that you have come into contact with. Promise your inner victim that you'll be more mindful of these personal attacks directed against the two of you and that you'll be angry and resentful together with your newfound friend.

### WARNING!

**AVOIDING THE FIFTH HABIT** leads to acceptance, peace of mind, and serenity. And the first step to overcoming our tendency to fall helplessly into the role of victim is to recognize how easily it is to do this and how powerful this urge can be in our lives. Let's admit it; we all, at some times and situations, enjoy playing the role of the victim. From a fairly early stage on, whether it was in interaction with our siblings or other kids in our neighborhood, we faced situations in which playing the victim was quite to our advantage. Often, our performance gained us the attention and sympathy we wanted. Often, it saved us a good throttling from our parents! We learned quickly that through playing the victim we could often manipulate people around us to come to our aid, that we could literally enlist persons to our side, but only if our performances were believable. And so we practiced our skills at playing the role of victim. Many of us got very, very good at this. We found this skill to be a very powerful tool in our repertoire of defense mechanisms.

We soon learned the importance of believability in becoming really good at playing the role of victim. Perhaps because of this, many of us began to believe that we really were in fact victims, that people and situations were really set up to conspire against us. The evidence for this was everywhere. It was there whenever we were frustrated in our desires and wishes. That was all the proof any of us needed to conclude in our minds that there must be a grand conspiracy trying to upend our goals and strivings. We became masters of concocting conspiracy theories in the most innocent situations that confronted us. The inner victim was born within us.

The problem is that many of us have had trouble recognizing and/or acknowledging this tendency in ourselves in adulthood. Sometimes being the victim is the path of least resistance in situations that we feel are overwhelming. At other times, we take on the role of victim unconsciously. It has become so natural to us that we would be shocked by the accusation that we were somehow allowing ourselves to be victimized. But, the truth of the matter is that we all, to varying degrees, are at times tempted to use the victim role in order to evade a difficult situation or dodge responsibility for some circumstance in our lives. By becoming a victim we take the burden of responsibility off our shoulders and expect others to come to our side, to our aid. Victims should be taken care of after all. Being a victim blinds us to any insight into our own part in creating a given undesirable situation.

Many people, however, enjoy playing the blame-game. In fact, for some, this can become a total approach to life. All events are seen as the result of someone or something's fault, never their own. Blame can always be tagged to somebody or something. To listen to such people can be a painful experience in itself. It's conceivable for a person to actually go through life seeing every negativity as somehow being the fault of someone else. And it's conceivable that a person could spend a lifetime helping such people and be a very successful and wealthy plaintiff attorney!

Playing the role of victim is often based on greater or lesser degrees of paranoia, the belief that someone or something is out to get us. When we realistically look at such paranoia we find that it's based on delusions of self-grandiosity and narcissism. Thinking that people or things are out to get us can only be based on the narcissistic belief that we're important enough that other people and institutions would waste their time being concerned with us! But the sad and obvious truth is this:

*Other people and institutions are too busy with their own existence to waste their time conspiring against us! Let's get real, folks! Other people have better things to do with their time!*

Lest any confusion be caused, I should state that I'm not so naïve as to think that there are not terribly tragic situations in which people are brutally victimized by other people. That is clear and those situations are self-evident. What I'm referring to here are those situations in which we presume ourselves to be and see ourselves as victims when, in reality, the evidence is just not there. I'm referring here to our quick tendency to use the victim role as a defense mechanism to exclude ourselves from any responsibility for a given situation or circumstance. As we'll see with the Sixth Habit in the next chapter, this game leads only to anger, resentment, and indignant self-righteousness. In other words, to more miserable living!

Catching ourselves assuming the role of victim and understanding the self-serving goals of such action allows us to stop in our tracks, reassess the situation, and see it in a truer, more authentic light. In such situations, the critical question becomes this: taking the actions of others out of the equation, what exactly was my part in bringing this event, situation, or circumstance to pass? What might I have done or not done to avoid this situation? What can I do now to change things for the better? Such questions lead to valuable insights into situations that might otherwise become the source of frustration, bitterness, and accusation.

Hopefully we will all take the more honest path and stop seeing ourselves as victims so that we can get on with living our lives with more peace of mind!

# 10

# The Sixth Habit:
# Resent the Unfairness!

The next step, referred to simply as the Sixth Habit, is certainly one of the most powerful tools for living miserably and with a great sense of malcontent. Like the First Habit (making yourself the center of the known universe, as you recall), this habit can also become a source of energy and fuel to help propel us into ever-increasing depths of misery. It can help to sustain us in those moments in which we might be tempted to look for other ways of understanding our lives, including those that might lead to a healthier attitude towards life. Like the power of narcissism tapped into by practicing the First Habit, the energy available by practicing this habit is boundless and sustainable, but it does require some training and practice. The power of the Sixth Habit derives from our anger and resentment.

We begin the Sixth Habit by practicing a few mental focusing exercises in which we examine the various aspects of our lives. We should closely examine all aspects of our lives, for example, our work, our family, our finances, our social status, our relationships, where we live, etc. Leave no stone unturned. Then as we focus on these various aspects of our lives, we think about ways in which each aspect could be much, much better. For example, think about how your work might involve fewer hours and higher pay. Or think about how you could really have a better wife, better friends, a better home, a better occupation. As we do this exercise, unlimited possibilities for exploration come to mind. In fact, we find, on close inspection, that most aspects of our present life situations could be better in some way or another. In some cases, it will be easy to visualize how certain aspects of our lives might be improved, and in other cases, it will require a bit of imagination. In either case, however, we should be able to find one or several ways in which our lives could be better. Remember: our imagination is one of the most powerful tools in our quest for misery, if properly used. Don't make the mistake of underestimating its power and usefulness. Otherwise, we run the risk of seeing our lives only from a realistic perspective.

Have you ever had the experience of going to a fancy restaurant and ordering a very nice dinner, but then, after seeing the entrees arriving at the adjacent table, you can't help thinking, "Darn it, I should have ordered what that guy ordered!" Sure, we've all at one time or another had this kind of "restaurant regret" experience. This experience contains the essence of practicing the Sixth Habit. In other words, with regard to all the various circumstances in our lives, the Sixth Habit encourages us to keep a watchful eye on the people around us, specifically looking for things that we wish we would have ordered! What once was only an occasional experience when dining out, now becomes a lifetime mindset!

Once we've considered all kinds of ways in which our present life could, in fact, be better, the next step is a bit trickier. The next step involves taking this overview of all the ways our lives could be better, and changing the *could* into a *should*. In other words, imagine all the reasons why your own life actually *should* be, in every way, just exactly the way you imagined it could be in the last step. Obviously, this step is trickier and will require even more imagination, maybe even a stretch of the imagination, in order to come up with convincing reasons for why one's life really should be different. But, as with many of the prior steps in developing the Habits, with a little practice, we will become ever more facile and skilled in quickly conceiving of the reasons why our lives should be better.

Before we move on to the next step in the process, a few words of caution are in order. As we think about the reasons that our lives should be different, we might stumble onto some reasons why our lives shouldn't be better. For example, say you imagined that your life could be better if you were a top executive at Microsoft Corp. instead of working for, say, a telemarketing company. You might at first be tempted to think something like, "Maybe I should have stayed in and finished high school after all" as a possible reason why you shouldn't be a top executive at Microsoft. Such a thought might give you pause to question the reasonableness of the life change you had imagined. Such thoughts, therefore, must immediately be countered by quickly thinking of a counter-argument to nip the previous thought in the bud. For instance, in our example, you could quickly remember that you heard once (substantiated or not) that many of the top executives at Microsoft Corp. never finished high school either but were just good buddies or family members of Bill Gates, before he hit it big! Immediately you can begin again to think, "Yea, that's right! I really could (and *should*) be a Microsoft millionaire!" It may take some quick thinking, but you should be able to come up with counter reasons like these should you find yourself up against anything, no matter how reasonable, which might stand in the way of your feeling justified in expecting your life to be different. This brings up another important principle we should discuss.

In the above example, you saw how you could avert a

situation in which you might be stumped and even come away feeling as if somehow your life might be just what it should be. But as the example illustrated, instead of getting stuck, you were able to come away with a sense that you actually deserved to be a top executive at Microsoft Corp. All it took was a different way of thinking about the situation, a different perspective, if you will, one that says, "Hey, why not me instead? Don't I got it coming to me?" It is this "Hey, I've got it coming to me" attitude that we are trying to foster here. What we're talking about is one of the fundamental and defining attitudes of the American people today: *the attitude of entitlement.*

We modern Americans, perhaps more so than any other people in the history of mankind have taken on an attitude of entitlement. We all feel that we are entitled to whatever the other guy is getting. I'm talking here about the attitude that doesn't merely consider whether one might be entitled to something, but rather the attitude that assumes the right of entitlement. Entitlement has everything to do with all the things that we "got coming to us", those things that we know we deserve. Things like government assistance and services, first-class no technology-held-back health care on demand, cheap gasoline, safe streets, farm subsidies, clean rest stops, easy to understand voting ballots, the right to bear arms (including armor-piercing rounds for those deer with really tough hides!), and must-see TV on Thursday nights. Anything and everything good in our lives is assumed to be a civic right, a deserved entitlement and, thus, taken for granted.

But perhaps the biggest entitlement of all involves the American tort system. Remember the case of the lady who spilled McDonald's hot coffee in her lap and sued McDonalds? You probably recall that she got something like $3 million for being clumsy and inept! Hey, what about the rest of us clumsy and inept folks? How come none of us has ever gotten rich as a direct result of our clumsiness? But this is just one example of the general attitude among Americans that if something adverse happens and someone suffers an injury or loss, someone must be at fault. Someone, that is, other than the persons themselves. And because someone else is responsible, we deserve to be compensated. Something bad happens and we deserve to be compensated for it. This is the ultimate entitlement attitude. Fortunately, the entire American legal system endorses this attitude and helps us live according to the Sixth Habit!

And thus we see the importance of the entitlement mentality in practicing the Sixth Habit. After we've identified the parts of our lives that should be better, we generate this entitlement mentality and soon we are convinced that we have been literally screwed out of all the things that we clearly deserve. Again, it may be helpful to look closely at someone else's circumstances that appear better than our own and then convince ourselves that that person has no more right to those circumstances than we do. This leads us directly into the final step of the Sixth Habit: developing a strong sense of the obvious unfairness in our lives and then feeling all the resultant anger and resentment. It's really quite simple too because all you need to do is ask yourself, "Hey, that other guy didn't really do anything more than what I could have just as easily done, yet look at that guy! The bastard's living in a double-wide!" or "Look at that guy with his own fancy bowling shoes and monogrammed bowling shirt! Damn guy's gotta flaunt it like he's frickin' Howard W. Hughes or something!" or "Look at that! Some thirteen-year-old snotty-nosed geek develops a web site with scatalogical humor, his company goes public, and now he's worth a gazillion dollars! It's just not fair!"

Believe me, with the television media and the Internet, there's no shortage of information sources available to us to identify all the many bastards out there who've got it so much better than we do! Just another modern miracle of living in the Information Age! With this limitless access to information, it's easy to find evidence of how unfair our own circumstances in life are. All we really need to do then is to identify a few pieces of evidence each day, dwell on these apparent evidences of injustice, and soon we'll know and experience anger, resentments, and general disgruntlement in our lives of a magnitude beyond what we ever thought was possible! And as we accumulate more and more evidence each day by comparing our circumstances with other people, the misery will continue to grow and grow indefinitely. The sky's the limit! Go for it!

Here are some exercises to help you get in touch with all of the unfairness with which your life is plagued.

## Daily Affirmations

1. Today I will compare my circumstances with those around me and look for evidence of injustice in my life.

2. I am a child of God, but for some (unfair) reason, He's got it out for me.

3. My life is not fair.

## Exercises

1. For each item below, write in the name of someone you know who has the same item, but a *much better one*. Be sure to identify someone who clearly does not deserve this better item as much as you do.

House_____

Car_____

Spouse_____

Children_____

Job_____

Health_____

Body_____

Garden_____

Home stereo system_____

Beanie Baby Collection_____

2. Each day try to write down five things that you deserved but didn't get. Keep the lists in a large binder. Go back to these lists and review monthly.

3. As you read the daily newspaper and listen to the evening news, pay special attention to any stories of undeserving people getting things that they shouldn't have. Write these down in a special journal entitled *The Lucky Undeserving Bastards Scorebook*.

## Meditation

Close your eyes and concentrate on your breathing. Imagine you're taking a trip, up and up into the clouds, higher and higher. See yourself entering heaven. Next visualize yourself face to face with the Supreme Creator of the Universe. If you're not religious, just imagine you're sitting across from Charlton Heston or James Cameron. Now imagine yourself describing to them all the unfair circumstances in your life and then asking them, "Why is my life so unfair, my circumstances so unjust?" Now imagine this God (or God substitute figure) replying to you, "Because I don't particularly like you! Deal with it." When you're ready, slowly come back to the room, drained emotionally, ready to continue your miserable day-to-day existence.

## WARNING!

**AVOIDING THE SIXTH HABIT** leads to gratitude. Gratitude is one of, if not the most, important ingredients for generating happiness and peace of mind. Gratitude is chased away by feelings of unfairness and an attitude of entitlement. And, as with all the habits of living miserably, we must first recognize, acknowledge, and look deeply into our quickness to fall into these habits, in this case our quick tendency to develop resentments regarding the perceived injustices in our lives. And who doesn't form such resentments? In truth, we all have thoughts at various times that the way the events of our lives play out is unfair. We feel that somehow the circumstances of our lives are more unfair relative to those of "others", but in reality the evidence of such claims is usually lacking. In reality, the only evidence of injustice exists in that space between our ears. And only in that space. It is the evidence we conjure up in our minds, created from faulty and misinformed perceptions of the true circumstances of those around us. We would all be happier and less angry if we could rid ourselves of such faulty thinking. But the first step in overcoming such faulty thinking is to recognize and admit our quick tendency to think in this way.

One might reasonably ask, where do these tendencies to

cry out, "Unfair!" come from, anyway? From whence comes this concept of justice and fairness? Consider this exchange:

*"Life is unfair!"*

*"Compared to what?"*

Compared to what? Can anyone come up with an appropriate response to this question? Perhaps the closest attempt at an answer would be, "Well, compared to a movie, a play, or a book in which every character gets their just reward or punishment." (at least according to our own limited idea of what would constitute fair consequences!) Isn't this really what we mean when we think that our life is in some way unfair, that some circumstance or event did not play out according to our script? And don't we all have our own internal screenplays entitled *The Wonderful, Exciting, And Fair Life of* (insert your name here)? And in truth, don't we all spend time and effort, to varying degrees, comparing our screenplay scripts with the reality of our lives? And to the extent that we believe in the universal fairness and validity of our individual scripts, we get all bent out of shape whenever our life doesn't play out according to our scripts. That's the point where we, in the role of director of the universe, scream out "All right, cut! Stop the camera! No, no! You've all got it wrong! Let's try it again, shall we? Places, everyone! Let's do another take!" But, of course, nobody else is quite as concerned about the great production of our life as we are (except of course, any serious co-dependants in our lives!)

If we truly examine deeply this "director's role" mentality in ourselves, it's not hard for us to laugh at the absurdity that underlies our feelings of unfairness. It really is quite laughable! Recognizing and laughing at our vain attempts to play the director makes it easier to step back and realize that we're not really in charge of this big production called our life! Often this insight alone can lead to the feeling that a huge burden has been lifted from our shoulders. Imagine the relief of understanding that one doesn't have to carry the responsibility of making sure that his or her life plays out according to his or her script! Along these same lines, I have always enjoyed a great definition of "life" I once heard:

*Life is that series of events that occur instead of what we expected or planned for.*

And even if we had come into this life with a promise or guarantee of fairness, do any of us really feel that we, armed only with our faulty and incomplete knowledge of the 'facts' at any given moment, would really be able to accurately ascertain or judge whether or not events in our individual lives were, in fact, fair or unfair? I seriously doubt it.

And so, we see that our tendency to want our lives to play out according to our own detailed scripts is a powerful and major source of misery, anger, and resentment. An alternative, healthier view would be to see our lives as great mysteries, adventures even, whose scripts were either not written yet, or if written, were kept secret from the actors (that would be us, folks!) in order to allow for the actors to improvise each scene using their own individual creativity. Such an attitude actually sounds kind of fun! What if that were, in fact, what life is, a large production of historical scale (God as director) in which our job were to respond to each moment of our lives with total spontaneity, total passion, and to savor every scene! As a friend of mine is fond of saying, "This life...it ain't no dress rehearsal!" And consider that if this were the case, how frustrated God would be! Imagine the work He had to do to set up this production and all He ends up with are millions of people running around with their own scripts, each trying to direct the action according to those scripts! And we actually wonder why God allows the existence of hurricanes, earthquakes, lawyers, and really bad family sit-coms!

For people who succeed in adopting a healthier, more spontaneous view of their lives, life is in fact, a mysterious but marvelous opportunity, a rare and short-lived opportunity to be on stage and to take part in this huge drama of mankind. Such an attitude makes one open to a wide range of possibilities, to any and all possibilities, really. Even tragic events are met with a kind of welcome openness. Such events are viewed as challenges to be overcome, challenges which, when overcome, bring gifts in the form of character. Such people throw out the notion of expected entitlements and would be hard-pressed to come up with any kind of list of things they deserved. Without an attitude of entitlement, they are able to see the gifts and blessings in their lives. This is true gratitude, being able to be genuinely surprised by everything good that comes one's way in life precisely because the notion that anything is deserved is seen as nonsense. In reality, the concept of entitlement is based only on fantasy and illusion. Let's face it, the concept of "deserving something" really only has relevance when discussing O.J. Simpson and lethal injection!

Angry resentments generated by our perceived sense of unfairness, and gratitude are mutually exclusive and cannot exist together in our heads. It's impossible. And so we must chose. Either we can continue to get frustrated when our list of the things we deserve isn't realized or we can realize the truth that "none of us got anything coming to us" and have an attitude of gratitude for all the things we do have. Once again, we have the choice of living in misery and discontent or living with peace of mind, happiness, and serenity. The choice is ours alone. And so, be careful out there, as they say, and chose wisely.

# 11

# The Seventh Habit:
# Gifts Are Nice, But Avoid
# The Present

At this point we're just about done with the Seven Habits. Assuming that you have been whole-heartedly applying all of the aforementioned habits in your life, you should now be experiencing new and profound levels of misery, frustration, and disgruntlement (if you happen to work for the U.S. Postal Service, remember: take it slow!) Despite the power of the first six habits in making your life miserable, it's important to point out that this last habit is every bit as important as the first six, perhaps even more important because, as we'll see, it ties in with the previous six habits quite well. So hang in there, dear reader, as we discuss the Seventh Habit.

The Seventh Habit deals entirely with the concept of time. Let's begin by briefly pondering the subject of time. Forget anything you've heard from theoretical physicists who talk about time being the fourth dimension or how space and time can be bent and all other such nonsense. Anyone who's ever tried to negotiate extra vacation days with a time-share representative knows that the concept of time being flexible or bendable is utter nonsense. Besides, these same physicists tell us that reality is composed of tiny super strings that exist in ten (or eleven) dimensions! Hello! Maybe these guys took one too many acid trips in college or something. I can tell you that I have definitely never seen anything even remotely like a super string, except maybe during that one Grateful Dead concert in 1973. And even in that case, I'm pretty sure it was part of the light show and besides, it couldn't have been in more than five dimensions. Six, tops!

Now, where were we? Oh, yes. Time. Anyone not subject to acid flashbacks understands that time is very simple. It consists of Past, Present, and Future and except when one is under the influence of marijuana or spending time with the in-laws, it seems to move along at a constant and invariable rate. Time moves from Past to Present to Future. Period. And regardless of what some idealistic Republican politicians might have you believe, there just ain't no going back to the 1950's, folks! Not physically possible. For any readers who might still cling to their childish science fiction fantasies of time travel, consider this fact: if time travel were possible, then someone certainly would have traveled back in time and say, realizing the tremendous financial potential of... oh say... computer operating software, would have stolen it from the original corporation that developed it, taken it and run with it, and consequently become the wealthiest man or woman on the planet! Under such an implausible scenario, most of the world's wealth would then be in the hands of a few ultra-wealthy individuals, perhaps even multi-billionaires, who could literally manipulate entire sectors of the economy through their huge multi-national corporations. Come on, folks! It's just too far-fetched to believe!

So it's clear that traveling back in time is not possible. Scientists have actually proven that the closest thing to time travel that modern technology has been able to achieve is to revive old fashion wear from the past. To their credit, however, scientists were able to bring back many of the silliest fashions of the 70's including bell-bottoms, tie-dye shirts, and shirts with zippers, a feat that many renowned scientists previously thought could never be achieved! Before we leave the general topic of time, a few more points should be made about time, all of which have been proven scientifically:

*A stitch in time saves nine* (I have never had any idea what the hell this saying means! How would one put a stitch in time! If any reader does understand this one, please send me an explanation).

*Time flies like an arrow, but fruit flies like a banana.* (Groucho Marx)

*Time keeps on slipping, slipping, slipping into the future* (although some theoretical physicists argue that it's more of a sliding action).

Time can, at times, be variable or relative: for example, in a doctor's office, the phrase "the doctor will be with you in a minute" can actually extend into several hours; and, of course, for a laptop computer battery that lasts "up to 12 hours," this time interval may shrink to 90 minutes or less.

The Seventh Habit basically admonishes us to avoid allowing ourselves to spend any part of our life in the present. One of the biggest threats to living a perfectly miserable life is allowing yourself to spontaneously relax and enjoy the present moment. Much has been written and said about living in the present moment, but this last habit will help ward off this last threat and allow our misery to continue full time, "24/7" as people are keen to say nowadays. The present moment, it turns out, is a very scary place to spend time because just about anything can happen. There is no control. Think about it for a moment. The Past can be remembered, the Future dreamed about, but the Present! It's a whole unpredictable can of worms. Finding yourself confronting the Present forces you to deal with reality and as everyone knows, reality is a very scary thing! The Seventh Habit tells us to just say no to the Present. Don't go there! Don't open the Present!

Since we're no longer going to waste any mental energy dealing with the Present, let's look at the advantages of the Past and the Future as our new safe abodes. First, the Past. What are the advantages of living in the Past? The Past could be thought of as the land of regrets and regrets, of course, are a wonderful source of misery. Think for a moment of all the memories from your past that you wish could have been different. Previously, you may have tended to let the Past go by without giving much thought to your regrets. But now, realizing that you're the center of the universe (First Habit), you understand that just about everything in your past could have been and should have been different. The Seventh Habit encourages us to dwell on any and all moments in the past and consider ways, whether dramatic or subtle, in which these moments could have been different, more to our liking and more in line with our needs and desires. It doesn't even require much of an imagination to dwell on countless ways in which the Past could have been different. Dwelling on these things will generate a world of regret about missed opportunities, the dreams and fantasies that never came true, that can now never come true, etc. And regret, as we've said, begats misery.

Now, you may be thinking at this point, "Gee, I could probably completely avoid the present moment by simply ruminating about my past. So why do I need concern myself with the Future?" You are actually correct in saying that a person could live entirely in the Past during his or her waking hours. But the Future provides another excellent place for your head to be as a means of avoiding the Present. And so it gives one a little variety. The important thing, of course, is that you

97

should avoid, at all costs, spending any time in the Present with its attendant risk of having to deal with reality.

The Future is the land of expectations and fears. We've already seen in Chapter Eight (Fourth Habit) how living in the Future can be a great means of generating fears. In addition to this, placing ourselves mentally in the Future can be a means of generating expectations. This is not to be confused with making goals, which can actually be healthy, but rather involves imagining entire scenarios of how one's life will go in the next several years, months, weeks, days, hours, or even minutes. The more detailed the expectations, the better. One should not limit this imagining to just those things concerning oneself, but rather should involve conceiving of entire detailed scenarios including other people's actions and responses, distant world events, acts of God, etc. You should come up with elaborate conceptions of your future, a screenplay, if you will, that could act as a guide to how everything and anything in your life should occur, in exact sequence, just as you see it in your mind's eye. Don't waste time wondering if some aspect of your future planning seems unrealistic or improbable. The more far-fetched and improbable your mental scenarios, the greater the potential for disappointment, resentment, frustration: all, of course, excellent sources of misery.

Let's now look at some exercises to help us learn to keep our minds out of the present moment by keeping our lives in the Past and in the Future.

## Daily Affirmations

1. Today I will refuse to accept "The Present"

2. Today I will not open or unwrap "The Present"

3. Today I will exchange "The Present" for "The Future" and "The Past"

## Exercises

1. List three things in your present moment that are very threatening to you or that you'd rather not have to deal with right now.

2. Write down three past experiences and then describe ways in which they might have been better. Then do the same thing for three people's past behavior and three past acts of God that had an adverse effect on you.

3. Write down a detailed scenario for tomorrow. Include events outside your control such as other people's behavior and their responses toward you. Tomorrow write down all the ways that your scenario did not come true. Finally, the day after tomorrow, list all the many resentments you've generated based on the lack of correlation between your imagined scenario and what actually happened.

## Meditation

Place yourself in a comfortable and relaxed position. Breathe regularly. Think about a recent event that didn't go the way you had imagined it would. Replay the scene in your mind, but this time imagine it the way you wanted it to transpire. Continue this imagery until you are convinced it really happened the way you wanted. Now relive the way it did happen and begin to feel the deep resentment toward yourself, other people, the unfair circumstances, all the things that caused the event to occur in ways contrary to how it should have occurred. Stay with these feelings of resentment until you feel that you might possibly spontaneously combust because of the intensity of these very feelings of anger and resentment. When you reach this point, slowly open your eyes and realize that you're back in the real world. Quickly get your mind back into worrying about the Past or dreaming about the Future and go about your daily activities, all the while maintaining your anger and resentment.

## WARNING:

**AVOIDING THE SEVENTH HABIT** will help you to live in the present moment. With practice, you will get better at identifying how prone you are to slip into thinking about regrets of the Past or into worrying about the Future. You will become better able to quickly catch yourself and recognize that you've allowed yourself to enter the illusory world of the Past or Future. You will be able to quickly remember that both the Past and the Future do not exist in reality. The Past is truly nothing more than memories, reinforced neural and synaptic patterns in your brain. The Future also has no reality except as a mental construct in your brain, an attempt to imagine something that has not come into existence yet. There is no way to predict the Future regardless of what you may have heard psychic expert Diane Warwick say on TV. Why? Because it hasn't happened yet! There is really only one time and one time only and that is the Present. Past and Future are not real things, just mental constructs. The present moment is not only real, it encompasses all of reality at each moment. Or you could say it defines reality. All reality is bound up within the present moment. Existence in the present moment is what defines something as real, as existent. There is no reality or existence separate from the Present. I know this goes against the logic of many a good science fiction movie or TV show, but that doesn't make it any less of a perfect truth. To believe anything else is just fanciful, wishful thinking that doesn't correspond to reality.

People who come to realize this fact, that only the Present is real, begin to live in the present moment. They give up idle thoughts of how the past could have or should have been different and instead keep their minds constantly in the Present. You can easily recognize people who have truly gained this insight. They are energetic, spontaneous, and alert. They seem to have an air of joyful acceptance of things as they are. They have few forehead creases because they view the Future as a mysterious source of limitless potential surprises and challenges, and they seem to be at ease in patiently waiting for it to unfold, in it's own time, at it's own pace. They understand that the Future will unfold naturally without their worrying about or fearing it. They also realize that the only way they can influence their individual future is by living fully awake in each present moment. They almost seem to view the next day as a child looks forward to Christmas on Christmas Eve, with a kind of eager anticipation. They understand that the entire value of the Future lies in its being the source of unknown numbers of "Presents".

People who understand the truth about the illusory nature of the Past understand that it's only value is as a source of learning experiences that help them live more fully and wisely in the Present. They realize the futility of regretting the Past. At the same time, however, they are able to honor its memory as a source of wisdom. In fact they see that past errors of judgement and behavior are actually far more valuable as teachers than their past successes. For this reason they have made peace with the Past rather than seeing it as a source of shame and regret. Someone once said, "Forgiveness is giving up all hope that the past could be any different than what it was" and in this way you could say that such people have truly forgiven themselves. They've come to peace with the concept of the Past as unchangeable.

People who have learned to stay in the present moment gain the gift of acceptance, which is perhaps, one of the greatest sources of peace of mind and serenity. They accept themselves, their strengths, weaknesses, other people, the circumstances of their lives, everything exactly as they are in this moment, right now! In this way, you could say they have traded worry, regret, shame, and fear for peace of mind and serenity, merely by changing the way they think about time and where they choose to spend their time. It's really quite miraculous when you stop to think about it, but you do have to stop and think about it. Stop, that is, at least long enough to pull your head out of the Past or Future!

# 12

# Avoiding the Seven Habits

In this final chapter, we will review both the Seven Habits and some of the ways we've learned to avoid them. You will recall that the major premise of this book is that the quickest path to happiness and peace of mind begins with an honest and thorough appreciation and acknowledgement of those very habits that most make us the miserable and discontented people we truly are (most of the time anyway!). It is only after such an honest and thorough recognition of the traits, mindsets, and habits that cause us all to get stuck in states of chronic misery that we are able to find the key to moving on to greater happiness and peace of mind. Before we review the Seven Habits, let's talk a little about happiness and peace of mind, as these are our real goals after all.

What is it we mean when we use the words "happiness" and "peace of mind"? What do these terms refer to? What kind of mental images pop into your mind when you hear these words? I'm sure for each of us different mental images come to mind depending on our particular past experiences. I remember seeing (and purchasing) a t-shirt that had what I thought was a very appropriate definition of happiness. "Happiness", it read, "is seeing your mother-in-law's photo on a milk carton" (beneath the word 'Missing'). But even this apparently relevant truth was wanting as I knew that even this seemingly perfect scenario might fail to bring me lasting happiness. There would always be a possibility that she might turn up! But seriously, the mental pictures that we summon up when we think of happiness are often rather vague, unreal, and nonspecific (i.e., seeing ourselves floating ethereally encased in soft white light!) or involve images of specific situations, situations that we somehow know would cause us to be instantly happy (i.e., winning the lottery). But both types of mental images are poor symbols of happiness and both miss the mark by a long shot.

Associating happiness with some kind of dreamy, hypnotic floating-through-the-air experience is pure fantasy, fueled by Hollywood imagery and MTV video productions. Rather than true happiness or peace of mind, such fantasies represent nothing more than delusional escapism and partly explain the high incidence of marijuana use everywhere. Associating happiness with such unreal images demonstrates that we have abandoned the possibility of ever experiencing happiness in our day-to-day real life experience. And hence we delegate the concepts of happiness and peace of mind to the realm of unreal dreamlike states. Many people even imagine an afterlife using such imagery but are often left wanting when they realize the incredible boredom associated with eternal states of absolute bliss. We can only endure so much happiness for so long and realize that we must eventually leave the theme park and head for the parking lot! By associating fulfillment with such fantasy mental states we're basically saying that we have given up all hope of achieving happiness and peace of mind in our lives and that we have surrendered to misery and accept it as the normal state of our everyday lives. "Better living through chemistry", by both legal and illegal means, then becomes a fairly rational, even justified, means of getting a temporary break from the perceived misery of the real world.

Equally misguided is the notion that happiness and peace

of mind are inseparably linked to the coming together of certain specific circumstances, usually detailed fantasies that are about as plausible as O.J. Simpson finding the "real killer." Such notions of happiness and peace of mind are misguided because they falsely assume that these feelings depend, not on one's mental attitude, but rather on external circumstances. By employing such notions of happiness, we then have, at least, very concrete and tangible "reasons" for why we feel so miserable most of the time. "After all, just look at all the ways the reality of my life is totally out of sync with my happiness and peace of mind model!" we might complain. Some might argue that at least with this model there is some hope, however unlikely, that circumstances will change and correspond more to the ideal circumstances that we have dreamed up. For some, perhaps, this hope is the only thing that allows them to continue tolerating their misery. But mentally linking states of happiness and peace of mind to external circumstances severely limits the possibility of us ever feeling happy or at peace. And why would we impose such limits on ourselves?

Assuming, then, that many of us falsely associate happiness with either unreal fantasy states or specific external circumstances, what then is the truth about happiness and peace of mind? What do we really know about these concepts, really? First, we must throw out all the false notions about them that we are prone to fall back on. We should realize that many of these fantasies are encouraged by the popular media of today, as we've already mentioned. Only after we've ridded ourselves of these unreal notions, can we look deeply into the reality of happiness and peace of mind. And we do know more about happiness and peace of mind than we might at first think. All of us have, after all, experienced real happiness at times in our lives. So, based on these experiences, what do we know?

Let's start with the obvious. When we experience peace of

mind or feelings of happiness, it feels really good. Plain and simple, it just feels good! If you imagine the last time you had such an experience, ask yourself the question: what happened next? Wasn't the pure experience of contentedness immediately followed by an awareness of those feelings with a thought like, "Hey, I'm feeling really good!" And then, almost effortlessly came the thought, "Hey, I don't want this to ever end!" And then what happened? It vanished, right? Sometimes instantly, sometimes slowly, but inevitably it leaves us. Scared off, you might say, by our conscious thoughts of trying to hold tightly to something that simply can't be held on to. It's akin to, as Alan Watts described it, trying to wrap up a cubic square foot of water with wrapping paper and string! And so we are inevitably frustrated because it feels really good but when we try to hold on to or control these feelings of contentedness, they mysteriously evade us. And this is where our brains really start to mess us up.

A more fruitful path to happiness, and peace of mind, it turns out, requires a paradigm shift (my apologies for using this exhausted, over-used catch phrase of the New Millenium!). Our brains, you see, are accustomed to a simple thought pattern that goes like this: I see, hear, experience something that is pleasurable, I want that thing, and then I actively pursue that thing. This mental pattern underlies most every kind of human activity from shopping to relationships and is the reason that Robert Downey Jr. is back in prison! But here's the catch. Happiness, by it's very nature, can't be obtained by direct pursuit. You can't go out and actively obtain or create true happiness or peace of mind! It can't be done! The harder you try, the more frustrated you are in your attempts. We have all experienced this truth, yet we cling to the concept that somehow it will be like other elements of our lives. "Perhaps we have just not been doing it right", we tell ourselves as we head naively down some other untried path with hopes of securing happiness and peace of mind. But the

106

reality is this: happiness and peace of mind always elude active attempts to obtain them. Like hunting monkeys while banging on drums!

If happiness and peace of mind cannot be obtained by active means, what's left? Only the indirect method. In other words, while happiness and peace of mind can't be approached directly, they do appear mysteriously and effortlessly when we actively let go of all the things that make us miserable! And so it's by way of an indirect method that we discover happiness. Instead of actively pursuing something or exerting ourselves toward some unobtainable goal, it involves rather the process of letting go of and surrendering ideas, illusions, fantasies, bad habits, mental thinking errors, and the like. Unfortunately, this concept is truly a paradigm shift that most of us are not likely to be very comfortable or familiar with. Most of us are much more skilled in the art of grasping and holding tightly on to things whether they be material possessions, relationships, habits, or whatever. None of us learned much about how to surrender in school, especially here in the land of the free and the home of the brave! Surrendering is for weaklings and cowards! And don't ask me to let go of something, regardless of what it is, if it's MINE!

But, like it or not, there's only one way to achieve happiness and peace of mind and that's by letting go of and giving up the very things that lead to our misery and discontent. That's the whole premise of this book. Identify the core things that most commonly lead us to misery, look at them honestly and deeply, and then, and this is of course the most difficult part, *let go of them*. And the only way to let go of them is to really understand how deeply they've become a part of us and how insidiously they lead to our misery and general unhappiness.

Let's review the Seven Habits, then, that lead to misery.

The First Habit involves acknowledging the power of our own narcissism and self-centeredness. At earlier points in human evolution, our innate self-centeredness was a valuable and necessary survival tool, but now it has become perhaps the major source of discontent and misery for most of us. It's been said that selfishness is a most peculiar disease because it causes everyone to be sick except the person who has it! But of course, this is really not true at all as it causes the most deadly spiritual sickness of all. Nobody wants to think of themselves as being selfish or self-centered, yet in reality we are all guilty of this crime! To some degree, we are all overly concerned with our own well-being and particular psychodramas! We tend to see our own concerns and problems as being somehow more important and tragic than similar situations involving other people (Saint Theresa, excused, of course!)

What are we to do with this natural tendency that contributes so powerfully to our misery? The worst approach, but unfortunately the most common approach, is to deny its existence or understate its power in our lives. Keep it hidden from external view but actively feed it and protect it in our inner life. What's the healthy alternative? To constantly recognize it whenever it rears its ugly head in our everyday lives! I'm not advocating, upon recognizing it, to loudly and publicly admit, "Hey, everyone! I just now felt I was the center of the universe!" An inner recognition is all that's necessary. And with such recognition comes an awareness of how ridiculous and pretentious such thoughts are. And consequently, there is only one thing to do: *LAUGH!* This is the ultimate weapon against narcissism, to laugh at it! Realizing how absurd it is for us to believe that our own concerns somehow have more gravity than anyone else's problems is cause for laughter! Laugh out loud, laugh to yourself, laugh long or laugh short, but laugh at yourself, for heaven's sake! For your happiness and your peace of mind's sake, *laugh.*

Recognizing the First Habit in ourselves is recognizing the truth that we all have a tendency to take ourselves too seriously. And the best way to avoid the First Habit is:

*Laugh at yourself whenever you catch yourself taking yourself way too seriously!*

The Second Habit has everything to do with powerlessness. We recognize that we are powerless over most aspects of our lives. In reality, we have control over just a few things: our thoughts, feelings, and behavior. Everything else is controlled by the natural forces of the universe or Bill Gates! The sooner we come to accept this fact of the universe, the sooner we'll be able to enjoy greater happiness and peace of mind. This Habit involves catching ourselves worrying about or trying to control something over which we have absolutely no control whatsoever. And such recognition should cause us to pause, re-evaluate, and then to laugh at ourselves for being foolish enough to concern ourselves with things outside our control. There is a great deal of peace of mind that comes from leaving all those things in the hand of the Supreme Creator and Bill Gates!

The Third Habit involves materialism and as we saw, materialism has nothing to do with how much stuff you own. Rather, it has to do with the extent to which your stuff owns you! The first step in avoiding this habit is to recognize our tendency to place our sense of security and our identity in our possessions. The power of this tendency determines the strength of the chains that bind us to our possessions. And the more bound we are to our possessions, the less freedom we really have. Catching ourselves using our material (or non-material) possessions to hide our inner insecurity, we can recognize how vulnerable our sense of ourselves really is, and therefore, laugh at ourselves! Once again, we see the incredible power of laughing at ourselves for our foolishness in trying to bolster our self-esteem through our possessions, which, by the way, have no lifetime guarantees!

The Fourth Habit identifies fear as a cause of much of our misery and unhappiness. This Habit ties in with the Third Habit through the concept of "The Heisman Trophy Principle". In the Buddhist faith, the two things that lead directly to suffering are desires and fears. We desire something and try to cling to it, but inevitably it's unavailable to us or taken away from us. Or we fear something and try, unsuccessfully, to push it away from us. And so, we are often just like the Heisman Trophy statue. You know, the football player grasping the football tightly in one arm while extending the other arm straight out to push away oncoming tacklers. This is a symbol of how we are during most of our lives, constantly trying to cling tightly to all the things we desire, all the while trying to push away all the things that we fear. Clinging to and pushing away, just like the Heisman Trophy guy! Fortunately, when we look deeply into the true nature of both our desires and our fears, we find that they are merely mental illusions and exist not in reality, but only in our minds. Both of them cause us a great deal of misery and unhappiness. For this reason, I find it helpful, whenever I'm feeling unhappy, frustrated, or depressed, to visualize the Heisman Trophy guy and ask myself, "O.K! What is it that I'm trying to cling to or push away?" Nearly always, I can identify either a desire or a fear that is at the root of my negative feelings. Then it's a simple matter of looking at whether or not those fears or desires correspond to the reality of the moment. In most cases, they do not but even when they do, it's much easier to understand and deal with these negative, uncomfortable feelings. And when I simply can't deal with these negative feelings, there's always Prozac! God love ya, Eli Lilly!

The Fifth and Sixth Habits fit naturally together. They

110

both have to do with the concept of fairness and how we respond to our perception of the unfairness of life. Here we have to stop and ask the question, where did this notion that life should be fair come from? Most of us probably picked this one up sometime between pre-school and sixth grade. This notion alone probably contributes to more misery than all the accordion music in the world! The funny thing is, we all would logically agree that none of us came into this world with a lifetime guarantee that our sojourn here would be "fair" in every way, yet how many of us cling to this notion so tightly throughout our lives? What's more, consider how easy it is for us to dismiss the unfair circumstances of people distantly (or not so distantly) removed from us, yet when we find ourselves faced with similar insults, we immediately expect a World Fairness Court to convene to right the obvious unfairness? These Habits ask us to recognize our quick tendencies to take this kind of a stance, see how ludicrous it is, and then, yes, to laugh at ourselves for the absurdity of such thoughts. This is also the best way to get out of the victim role and spare ourselves the misery that stems from resentment of the unfairness of life.

The Seventh Habit identifies another major thinking error that causes tremendous misery, or perhaps more accurately stated, prevents us from experiencing happiness and peace of mind. One of the truths about happiness and peace of mind that is undeniable, is that they can exist only in the present moment. If your head is in the past, you can only experience memories of happiness, but never actual happiness. Similarly, if your head is in the future, you can experience fantasies about future happiness, but never actual happiness. Happiness and peace of mind exist only in the present moment. Unfortunately, most of us spend inordinate amounts of our life languishing in memories of past moments of happiness or tirelessly trying to plan for future happiness, never realizing that we've thereby essentially denied ourselves any hope of experiencing actual happiness. The only chance for the actual experience is to remove our heads from the past and future, and keep it in the only sphere of reality where peace of mind and happiness can exist, namely the present moment.

So there you have it, the Seven Habits of Highly Miserable People. I absolutely guarantee that if you'll keep a constant and vigilant watch for these habits popping up in your everyday life, identify them, recognize their lack of correspondence to reality and thereby laugh at yourself, you'll live a much happier, joyful, and fulfilling life. Or at least one with more laughter, which is always a good thing. And if you try it and find that you are not happier, at least more of the time, then you always have the option of going back to the status quo of taking yourself too seriously, trying to control things you can't, pursuing mindless possession of more stuff, living in fear, playing the role of victim as you resent all the unfairness in your life, never able to stop regretting your past mistakes or worrying about future catastrophes. Not a very good alternative, is it? The choice is yours. Choose wisely!

If you enjoyed this book, why not send a copy to a friend? If you didn't enjoy it why not send a copy to someone you dislike? Either way, it's the perfect gift! To obtain a copy, go to www.writerspress.com. Also check out the author's website at www.giveone.com. Comments and suggestions are welcomed. Send them by e-mail to mborup@micron.net.

0-595-24709-1

Printed in the United States
136935LV00003B/44/A